HERBAL
REMEDIES
IN POTS

HERBAL
REMEDIES
IN POTS

Effie Romain and
Sue Hawkey, MNIMH

DK

DORLING KINDERSLEY
LONDON • NEW YORK • STUTTGART • MOSCOW

A DORLING KINDERSLEY BOOK

Project Editor Heather Jones

Art Editor Glenda Tyrrell

Managing Editor Maureen Rissik

Managing Art Editor Philip Gilderdale

Production Manager Maryann Rogers

Photographer Steve Gorton

Authors' dedication
For Daisy Hawkey and the Bells

First published in Great Britain in 1996 by Dorling Kindersley Ltd
9 Henrietta Street, London WC2E 8PS

A CIP catalogue record of this book is available from the British Library.

ISBN 0 7513 0295 3

Reproduced by Colourscan, Singapore

Printed and bound by Toppan, Singapore

CONTENTS

INTRODUCTION

This book is intended to help you discover the pleasure of growing some of the common medicinal herbs and to feel confident about using them in tonics or as simple remedies to treat your own, or your family's, minor health problems.

REDISCOVERING MEDICINAL HERBS

Our forebears used herbs to treat every ailment; they had an intimate knowledge of medicinal herbs and passed this on to subsequent generations. With the advent of modern medicine, this knowledge has largely been lost. Today, some of the most therapeutic herbs, such as docks and nettles that bring health-promoting minerals from deep down in the soil, are thought of only as rampant weeds, and unwelcome in the garden. Growing such plants in containers helps restrain their invasive properties, while allowing herbs that treat a particular ailment to be grouped for ease of gathering and to be grown by those with limited space.

GROWING HERBS

All the herbs in this book can be grown outdoors in temperate zones (make sure pots are frost proof to prevent cracking in winter). Some, particularly the culinary herbs, are widely available from garden centres. Many of the others are commonly found growing wild in the countryside, and can also be bought as plants from herb specialists listed in local classified directories. Any plant that is difficult to come by can usually be bought as seed.

Medicinal herbs should be in good condition and gathered at the peak of their potency. They should be planted in well-prepared soil, and watered and fed regularly with organic plant food (p.84). Keep a daily watch for pests: spray aphids with soft soap, and pick off slugs and snails. Never use insecticides on herbs that are intended for ingestion.

Annuals and perennials should be bought as small plants, or grown from seed. Some perennials benefit from being left in the pot to mature for a further season; shrubs can thrive for years. Even if you wish to retain shrubs and perennials, clear out the pot in winter, trim tangled roots, and replant with some fresh compost.

MAKING HERBAL REMEDIES

Each of the 34 pots featured in this book is planted with herbs to treat a common ailment or to provide a tonic. All the recipes can be made safely at home, using standard kitchen equipment. Step-by-step photographs (pp.88–92) show how to make herbal preparations such as teas, decoctions, syrups, oils, and ointments. Never exceed the dosages given for each remedy: if symptoms persist, consult a medical practitioner or herbalist.

PROPAGATING AND STORING HERBS

At the end of the growing season, use the propagation instructions and the checklist on page 93 to help you decide whether to propagate a plant, retain, or compost it. To make the most of your herbs, gather and dry them during the growing season (p.86), and store for all-year-round use. If you find a suitable remedy but can't grow enough of a particular herb for your needs, supplement your supply with dried material from a herbalist shop. Be careful of harvesting from the wild: legally, in most countries, you can pick only aerial parts; make sure they have not been sprayed with insecticides and are unpolluted.

KEY TO SYMBOLS USED ON PAGES 10–77

Remedy methods		Plant parts used
Tea or infusion	Gargle	Leaves
Syrup	Drops	Fruit
Decoction	Compress	Flower
Tincture	Wash	Aerial parts
Infused oil	Fresh leaves	Bulb
Ointment	Fresh roots	Seeds
Cream	Seeds	Root
		Bark

SOME RESTRICTED HERBS

AUSTRALIA AND NEW ZEALAND
Some plants mentioned in this book are considered serious weeds in New Zealand and Australia. Contact your local authority for a listing of plants that are considered noxious in your area.

HERBAL
REMEDY POTS

*The 34 pots on pages 10–77 are planted
with herbs that treat common ailments.
Here are planting and growing
instructions, information about each herb
and its therapeutic uses, and a selection
of remedy recipes for each ailment.*

SORE THROATS, COUGHS, AND COLDS

The herbs used here contain volatile oils that clear the nose, throat, and chest. Sage also has a drying effect on inflamed mucous membranes. The thymes and elecampane help eliminate sticky mucus and combine with ground ivy and hyssop to relieve catarrh.

POT INFORMATION

Herbs

Purple sage
Salvia officinalis
'Purpurascens'

Hyssop
Hyssopus officinalis

Lemon thyme
'Silver Queen'
Thymus x
citriodorus
'Silver Queen'

Lemon thyme
Thymus x citriodorus

Elecampane
Inula helenium

Ground ivy
Glechoma hederacea

Suggested pot

50cm (20in)

47cm (19in)

Planting and feeding

- 92 litres compost
- Standard or organic plant food

CULTIVATION

START by buying one purple sage, one hyssop, and three thymes as plants from a garden centre or herb specialist. Buy two elecampane plants and two ground ivy plants from a herb specialist.
POSITION in a sunny spot.
WATER daily in hot, dry weather.
FEED every two weeks in summer.
MAINTAIN the shape of purple sage, hyssop, and thymes by trimming regularly.

GATHER aerial parts of purple sage, hyssop, thymes, and ground ivy throughout the growing season. Dry for winter use. Harvest elecampane root in autumn.
PROPAGATE sage and hyssop from cuttings (p.82). Propagate thymes and elecampane by dividing in autumn (p.83). Clear out the mass of ground ivy each year but keep a few healthy pieces of stem with roots and replant in the pot.

REMEDY RECIPES

Sage gargle CAUTION (see opp.)
Make a strong tea (p.88) with a handful of sage leaves. Add a little honey. Allow to cool. Strain, and gargle often.

Anti-catarrhal tea
Make a standard tea (p.88) with thyme, ground ivy, and hyssop. Drink at the onset of a cold or when you have catarrh.

Syrup for a cough
Heat 400g (12oz) sugar in 500ml (17fl oz) water until dissolved. Add two chopped elecampane roots. Heat gently. When a menthol scent is evident, add a handful of hyssop. Cook for two more minutes. Remove from the heat and leave to cool. Strain, bottle, and store. Take one teaspoonful three times a day.

Elecampane
The roots of this herb have a clean, fresh aroma. Just a whiff will help clear your chest.

Hyssop
A pretty plant with pink or blue flowers, hyssop should stay in flower throughout the summer if trimmed.

Purple sage
Sometimes referred to as red sage, this plant grows well in containers.
CAUTION
• Avoid if epileptic.
• Avoid high doses if pregnant.

Lemon thyme 'Silver Queen'
A recent variety of lemon thyme, 'Silver Queen' adds a lightness to the pot.

Lemon thyme
The lemon scent and silvery leaves of lemon thyme make it a good alternative to common thyme.

Ground ivy
Covered with aromatic lavender-blue flowers in spring, ground ivy was once the main ingredient used to flavour ale.

FEVERS AND 'FLU

These herbs treat the symptoms associated with fevers and 'flu.
False indigo combats infection and purple coneflower mobilizes the
body's natural defences. Plantain is astringent, reducing catarrh,
while yarrow aids the passage of fevers by encouraging perspiration.

POT INFORMATION

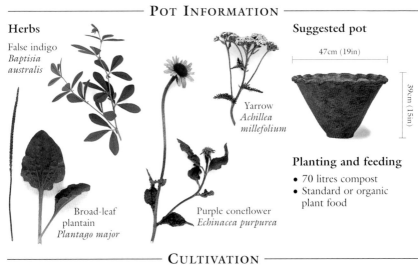

Herbs

False indigo
Baptisia
australis

Yarrow
Achillea
millefolium

Broad-leaf
plantain
Plantago major

Purple coneflower
Echinacea purpurea

Suggested pot

47cm (19in)

39cm (15in)

Planting and feeding

- 70 litres compost
- Standard or organic
  plant food

CULTIVATION

START by buying two purple coneflower plants from a garden centre. Buy a good-sized false indigo plant, a yarrow, and a plantain plant from a herb specialist.
POSITION in a sunny spot.
WATER daily. Don't let the yarrow dry out.
FEED with a dilute solution every two weeks from early summer onwards.
MAINTAIN by deadheading false indigo, coneflower, and plantain.

GATHER aerial parts of yarrow and plantain when the plant is in flower. Dry for winter use. Harvest and dry roots of coneflower and indigo in autumn.
PROPAGATE plantain by detaching a few plantlets from around the parent and replant (p.83). Replant rooted stems of yarrow (p.83). Divide coneflower and indigo when they are mature enough to provide plants for the following year (p.83).

REMEDY RECIPES

 Tea for a head cold
CAUTION (see opp.)

Most fevers and 'flu strike in winter, so it is best to dry plenty of these herbs in summer (pp.86–7). Make a standard tea (p.88) with a teaspoon of dried plantain and a teaspoon of dried yarrow to a cup of boiling water. Take three or four times a day, as long as symptoms persist.

 Decoction for 'flu
CAUTION (see opp.)

Make a decoction (p.89) with four teaspoons of dried purple coneflower root and two teaspoons of dried false indigo root to 600ml (1 pint) water. Strain and leave to cool. Take one cupful, either hot or cold, four times a day during a bout of 'flu.

Yarrow
Yarrow's generic name
Achillea is said to derive
from Achilles, the Greek
hero who used the herb to
staunch battle wounds.
CAUTION
• Can cause skin rashes.
• Avoid large doses in
pregnancy.

Purple coneflower
Indigenous to the United
States, purple coneflower
is a powerful immune
system stimulant.

False indigo
This pretty plant has blue
lupin-like flowers.
CAUTION
Large doses can cause
nausea, diarrhoea, and
vomiting.

Broad-leaf plantain
With its ribbed leaves
and upright flower
heads, broad-leaf
plantain looks very
striking in a pot.

WINTER CHILLS

The two herbs in this pot, horseradish and nasturtium, are both rich in vitamin C, which helps the body resist infection. They also contain stimulating and anti-infective, mustard-like oils which make them useful for staving off winter colds and chills.

POT INFORMATION

Herbs

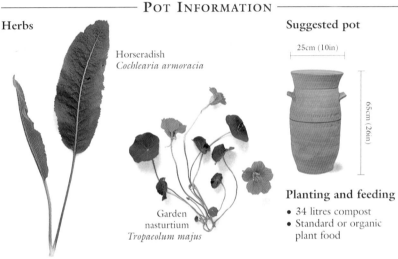

Horseradish
Cochlearia armoracia

Garden
nasturtium
Tropaeolum majus

Suggested pot

25cm (10in)

65cm (26in)

Planting and feeding
- 34 litres compost
- Standard or organic plant food

CULTIVATION

START by buying one horseradish plant from a herb specialist in spring. Scatter a few nasturtium seeds on the surface of the pot in early spring or buy four or five plants from a garden centre. Horseradish needs a tall pot because of its deep roots.
POSITION in a sunny spot.
WATER daily in hot, dry weather.
FEED every two weeks.
MAINTAIN by trimming the horseradish leaves if they get too straggly. Deadhead

nasturtium to encourage flowering. Nasturtium is prone to black-fly infestation: treat any by spraying immediately with a solution of soft soap.
GATHER aerial parts of nasturtium during the season. Use or freeze (p.86). Harvest horseradish root in autumn (p.87). Store.
PROPAGATE horseradish by root cuttings (p.83) in autumn. Let a few nasturtium flowers go to seed and keep the seed for planting the following year.

REMEDY RECIPES

Horseradish drink for a chill
To store horseradish, scrub and peel root. Chop finely or grate. Pack loosely into a jar. Add a little salt, and cover with white vinegar. Seal. When needed, add one teaspoon to a cup of hot water and drink three times a day.

Nasturtium tea for a cold
Because they are so delicate, nasturtium flowers are better frozen than dried. To ease colds, add a handful of frozen flowers and leaves to half a litre (1 pint) of boiling water. Drink one cupful three times a day during a cold.

❋ ◈ Nasturtium

With bright orangey-red flowers, these plants give a colourful display and are very easy to grow from seed. The name comes from the Latin for "nose twister".

❋ Horseradish

The handsome, dark-green leaves of this herb compensate for its reluctance to flower in a container.

Horseradish root
Two clay drains, cut across the middle, can be used to reveal the root without disturbing the plant.

15

INDIGESTION

Peppermint is known throughout the world for its digestive properties. Mugwort stimulates the digestive juices, while marsh mallow soothes the intestines. Meadowsweet has aspirin-like constituents and also contains tannins which protect the stomach lining.

POT INFORMATION

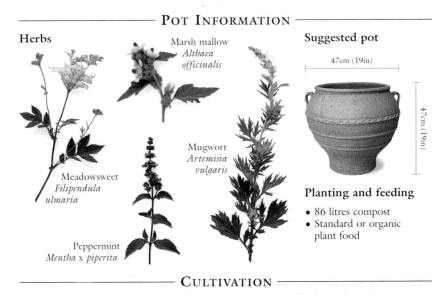

Herbs

Marsh mallow
*Althaea
officinalis*

Meadowsweet
*Filipendula
ulmaria*

Mugwort
*Artemisia
vulgaris*

Peppermint
Mentha x *piperita*

Suggested pot

47cm (19in)

47cm (19in)

Planting and feeding

- 86 litres compost
- Standard or organic plant food

CULTIVATION

START by buying two peppermint plants from a garden centre. Buy one each of the remaining plants from a herb specialist.
POSITION in partial shade.
WATER daily in hot, dry weather.
FEED monthly from mid-summer.
MAINTAIN by trimming topmost leaves of mugwort to stop it from growing too tall. Use peppermint regularly in tea.

GATHER aerial parts of meadowsweet, peppermint, and mugwort as needed. Harvest marsh mallow root in autumn.
PROPAGATE mugwort and peppermint from a few healthy, rooted pieces of stem (p.83). Replant in the container. In autumn, divide root ball of meadowsweet and, if the plant is mature enough, divide marsh mallow (p.83).

REMEDY RECIPES

After-dinner tea
As a pleasant digestive after a meal, make a pot of tea (p.88) with a handful of peppermint leaves.

Indigestion tea CAUTIONS (see opp.)
Make a tea (p.88) with a sprig of meadowsweet, mugwort, and peppermint. Sip one or two cupfuls a day.

Soothing marsh mallow syrup
A syrup is a very suitable medium for this mucilaginous plant. Soak about 12cm (5in) of cleaned, chopped root in 500ml (17fl oz) water overnight. Add 250g (8oz) sugar. Heat and stir until dissolved. Simmer for 10 mins. Strain, bottle, and store. To soothe irritation in the gut, take one teaspoonful as needed.

Mugwort
*This is one of the most
common hedgerow plants.*
CAUTION
*Do not use if
pregnant or
breastfeeding.*

Marsh mallow
*The gelatinous roots
of this plant, which
is closely related to
the hollyhock, were
used to make the
original marsh-
mallow confection.*

Meadowsweet
*Found freely growing
along the banks of streams
and ditches, this plant has
clusters of tiny cream flowers.
Its roots smell like an old-
fashioned chemist shop.*
CAUTION
Avoid if allergic to aspirin.

Peppermint
*Like all the mint
family, peppermint
has an invasive habit
in the garden, but can
be restrained in a pot.*

CONSTIPATION

*These plants will keep reluctant bowels active. Flax seed is a bulk
laxative, stretching and lubricating the gut wall. Dock roots encourage
evacuation, while at the same time improving digestion.
Peppermint and Roman chamomile relax the bowel.*

POT INFORMATION

Herbs

Curled dock
Rumex crispus

Flax
*Linum
perenne*

Roman
chamomile
*Chamaemelum
nobile*

Peppermint
Mentha x *piperita*

Suggested pot

40cm (16in)

39cm (15in)

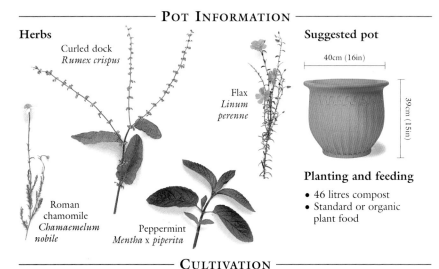

Planting and feeding

- 46 litres compost
- Standard or organic
  plant food

CULTIVATION

START dock from seed (p.80) bought from
a herb specialist. Plant two in the pot. Buy
two peppermint, two Roman chamomile, and
five flax plants from a garden centre (German
chamomile can also be used, see p.26).
POSITION in a sunny spot.
WATER every two or three days.
FEED monthly in summer.
MAINTAIN by deadheading Roman
chamomile. Use peppermint regularly in

tea. After collecting flax seed for use
in remedies, cut down dead stems.
GATHER chamomile flowers and aerial
parts of mint as needed. Harvest dock root
in autumn. Collect flax seed as it ripens.
PROPAGATE dock and chamomile by
detaching small plantlets and replanting in
the pot (p.83). Propagate mint from rooted
pieces of stem (p.83). Keep a few flax seeds
and sow for plants in spring.

REMEDY RECIPES

Flax seed laxative
Put one or two tablespoons of
seed in a cup. Add half a cup of cold
water and leave seed to swell and soften.
Drink before breakfast. For a milder
effect, add half a tablespoon of seed
to a portion of muesli. Flax seed also
contains essential fatty acids. It is safe
to use this remedy over several months.

Dock root laxative
Make a decoction (p.89) with one
teaspoon of dock root to one cup of water.
Drink three times a day as needed.

Anti-spasmodic tea
Make a tea (p.88) with a few
chamomile flowers and a peppermint
sprig. Strain and drink three times a day.

Flax
Also known as linseed, this is a fragile, airy plant with slender stems and flat, purple-blue flowers.

Curled dock
Because of its invasive nature, the dock is not a well-loved plant but its long roots bring up minerals from deep down in the soil.

Peppermint
All varieties of mint are therapeutic but peppermint, with its purple-tinged, dark-green leaves, is one of the best to grow for its strong taste and scent.

Roman chamomile
This is the perennial chamomile. Its leaves are strongly aromatic. When crushed, they smell of fresh apples, and it is this species that is used for chamomile lawns.

DIARRHOEA

*Containing tannins like those present in Indian tea, all these herbs
have a drying action, which calms and slows intestinal activity. All
four are tonics, but great burnet and Solomon's seal also provide
nourishment, which is helpful for digestive upsets.*

POT INFORMATION

Herbs

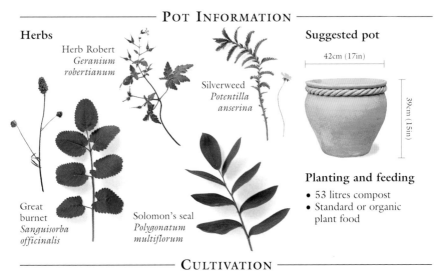

Herb Robert
*Geranium
robertianum*

Silverweed
*Potentilla
anserina*

Great
burnet
*Sanguisorba
officinalis*

Solomon's seal
*Polygonatum
multiflorum*

Suggested pot

42cm (17in)

39cm (15in)

Planting and feeding

• 53 litres compost
• Standard or organic
  plant food

CULTIVATION

START by sowing great burnet, silverweed,
and herb Robert seed (p.80), bought from
a herb specialist. Plant two of each. Buy two
Solomon's seal plants from a garden centre.
POSITION in semi-shade.
WATER daily in hot, dry weather.
FEED every two weeks from mid-summer.
MAINTAIN by cutting back dead stems of
Solomon's seal a month after flowering. To
do so any sooner will starve the rhizome.

GATHER aerial parts of silverweed, great
burnet, and herb Robert as needed. In
autumn harvest root of Solomon's seal
and great burnet for use (p.87).
PROPAGATE silverweed by detaching
a few plantlets (p.83). Divide great burnet
(p.83) and sow seed of herb Robert. New
"buds" will have formed on the Solomon's
seal rhizomes. For plants next year, cut
out budded sections and pot up.

REMEDY RECIPES

Anti-diarrhoea tea
Add a sprig of herb Robert, great
burnet, and silverweed to a cup of boiling
water. Drink three times a day, as needed.

Fresh root of Solomon's seal
Solomon's seal is described by
herbalists as "healing and sealing". The
root contains nutritious starches and

can be eaten raw like a vegetable.
Unearth a couple of roots, clean them,
and chew during an attack of diarrhoea.

Anti-diarrhoea decoction
Make a standard decoction
(p.89) with root of great burnet or
Solomon's seal. Drink a cupful three
times a day, as needed.

Great burnet
The leaves of great burnet taste slightly like walnuts and they make a pleasant addition to salads.

Herb Robert
A delicate annual, herb Robert is very liberal with its seeds. Its foliage turns an attractive red in autumn or in drought.

Solomon's seal
In spring, creamy-white pendent flowers hang from each leaf axil. Growing Solomon's seal in a container makes it easier to control the inevitable infestation of sawfly caterpillar.

Silverweed
This lovely plant gets its name from its silvery green foliage. Herbalists maintain that a leaf placed in a shoe will relieve aching feet.

IRRITABLE BOWEL SYNDROME

These plants each treat a different aspect of this condition. Roman chamomile and lemon balm are relaxing and anti-inflammatory; chamomile can also reduce allergic reactions. Agrimony is a general digestive tonic, while marigold is healing and anti-fungal.

POT INFORMATION

Herbs

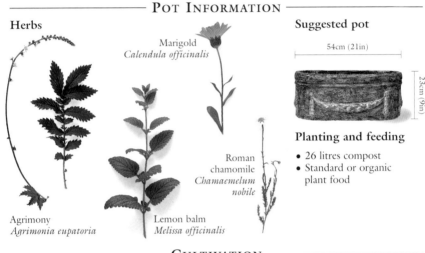

Marigold
Calendula officinalis

Roman
chamomile
*Chamaemelum
nobile*

Agrimony
Agrimonia eupatoria

Lemon balm
Melissa officinalis

Suggested pot

54cm (21in)

23cm (9in)

Planting and feeding

- 26 litres compost
- Standard or organic
  plant food

CULTIVATION

START by buying two plants each of Roman chamomile and lemon balm from a garden centre. Buy two agrimony plants from a herb specialist. Marigold can be bought as pot plants or grown from seed. Plant two.
POSITION in a sunny spot.
WATER daily in hot, dry weather.
FEED monthly in summer.
MAINTAIN by trimming lemon balm. Deadhead marigold and chamomile.

GATHER chamomile and marigold flowers as they appear. Pick aerial parts of lemon balm and agrimony as needed.
PROPAGATE lemon balm from pieces of rooted stem (p.83). In autumn collect marigold seeds and resow for plants next spring (p.80). Propagate Roman chamomile by detaching a few plantlets and replanting in the pot (p.83). Propagate agrimony by dividing the root ball (p.83) in autumn.

REMEDY RECIPES

Calming chamomile tea
Make a strong tea (p.88) with three teaspoons of fresh flowers, or two of dried, per cup of boiling water. Strain and drink three times a day, as needed.

Bowel tonic tea
Make a tea (p.88) with chamomile and marigold flowers and aerial parts of

agrimony and lemon balm. Use two teaspoons mixed fresh herbs or one of dried to a cup of water. Drink regularly.

Relaxing tea
Make a tea (p.88) with a handful of lemon balm and a few chamomile flowers to 600ml (1 pint) water. Steep, strain, and drink three times a day.

✿ ✿ **Lemon balm**
This herb is available in a variegated form but M. officinalis *is more potent and, with its deep-green foliage, looks more attractive in a container.*

✿ **Agrimony**
Tall, elegant, yellow flower stems of agrimony grow from a woody root. The serrated leaves contain vitamins B and K.

✿ **Marigold**
Marigold flowers have a fresh, clean scent and leave a sticky orange-yellow resin on the hands when picked.

✿ **Roman chamomile**
The beneficial effects of chamomile on the digestive system have been known to herbalists since ancient times, earning it the name "mother of the gut".

HAEMORRHOIDS

Also known as piles, haemorrhoids are varicose veins in the rectum wall. Celandine and witch hazel are both astringent and will help shrink piles. Marigold helps reduce inflammation, while peppermint has a slight anaesthetic effect and will relieve discomfort.

POT INFORMATION

Herbs

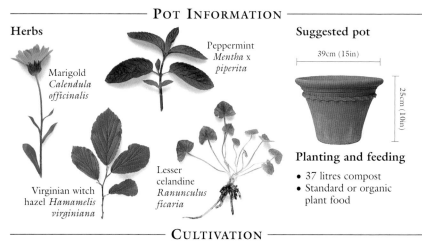

Marigold
Calendula officinalis

Peppermint
Mentha x
piperita

Virginian witch
hazel *Hamamelis
virginiana*

Lesser
celandine
*Ranunculus
ficaria*

Suggested pot

39cm (15in)

25cm (10in)

Planting and feeding

- 37 litres compost
- Standard or organic plant food

CULTIVATION

START by buying a witch hazel plant from a shrub or herb specialist. Grow lesser celandine from seed bought from a herb specialist. Buy two peppermint plants from a garden centre. Grow marigolds from seed or buy six young plants.
POSITION in a sunny spot.
WATER regularly and daily in hot, dry weather. Don't let the witch hazel dry out.
FEED weekly in summer with a dilute feed – about half as strong as any recommended dilution.

MAINTAIN by deadheading marigold and pinching out growing points of witch hazel.
GATHER aerial parts of peppermint and leaves of witch hazel as required. Collect witch hazel bark when woody enough. In summer, unearth celandine roots. Collect marigold flowers as they appear.
PROPAGATE marigold by collecting and sowing seed (p.80). Propagate mint from a few rooted pieces of stem (p.83). Remove all but two celandine roots. Leave witch hazel for about three years, then divide.

REMEDY RECIPES

Pile ointment CAUTION (see opp.) Marigold, celandine, and witch hazel can be made into an ointment using petroleum jelly or a base cream (p.92). Chop up the witch hazel bark and the celandine root and add to the cream. Use one tablespoon of root and bark to each 100g (3½oz) of cream. Add four fresh or dried marigold flowers and

heat gently for 15 mins. At the last moment, add a sprig of peppermint. Strain into jars. Use as needed.

Tea to help piles
To treat the condition internally, make a standard tea (p.88) with marigold flowers and witch hazel leaves. Drink a cupful three times a day, as needed.

Virginian witch hazel
Considered to be the best wood for making divining rods, witch hazel has small, yellow, delicately scented flowers that appear in autumn on bare stems.

Marigold
Excellent for healing the skin, this cheerful hardy annual was valued by the ancient Egyptians as a rejuvenating herb.

Peppermint
Peppermint is used to flavour many familiar products such as toothpaste and chewing gum. It is cooling and refreshing, and helps to settle the stomach.

Lesser celandine
Also known as pilewort, this is one of a number of plants that holds a visual clue to the condition it cures: its knobbly roots resemble haemorrhoids.
CAUTION
Avoid if pregnant.

TENSION

These herbs each promote relaxation in a different way. Skullcap helps calm mental agitation, while betony relieves anxiety and tension headaches. German chamomile and lemon balm relax nervous stomach, and lavender lifts the spirits.

POT INFORMATION

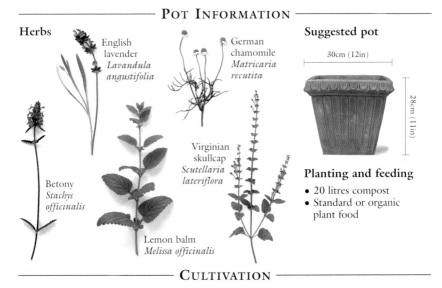

Herbs

English lavender
Lavandula angustifolia

German chamomile
Matricaria recutita

Betony
Stachys officinalis

Virginian skullcap
Scutellaria lateriflora

Lemon balm
Melissa officinalis

Suggested pot

30cm (12in)

28cm (11in)

Planting and feeding
- 20 litres compost
- Standard or organic plant food

CULTIVATION

START by sowing chamomile seed (p.80), bought from a herb specialist. Plant two in the container. Buy one lemon balm, two skullcap, two betony, and three lavender plants from a herb specialist.
POSITION in a sunny spot.
WATER daily during hot, dry weather.
FEED monthly during the summer.
MAINTAIN by trimming lemon balm and lavender. Deadhead chamomile.

GATHER chamomile flowers as they appear. Pick aerial parts of betony, skullcap, and lemon balm as needed. Pick lavender just before the flowers open.
PROPAGATE lavender from cuttings (p.82) and lemon balm from rooted pieces of stem (p.83). Detach plantlets of betony and divide skullcap (p.83). Collect seed of chamomile in autumn and sow for plants in spring (p.80).

REMEDY RECIPES

Tea for nervous exhaustion
To ensure a peaceful sleep, make a tea (p.88) with a handful of chamomile flowers and a small sprig of lavender per cup of boiling water. If fresh herbs are not available, use one teaspoon of dried herbs. Strain and drink three times a day over a period of several weeks.

Calming tonic tea
Make a pot of tea (p.88) with a sprig each of aerial parts of betony, skullcap, and lemon balm, plus one lavender flowerhead. Fill the pot with boiling water. Drink a cup of this tea, hot or cold, three times a day, especially if you are feeling anxious.

✼ Betony
*With dark-green leaves
and spikes of lilac-pink
flowers, betony combines
well with the other
plants in this pot.*

✼ Lemon balm
*A bushy plant, with
lemon-scented foliage
and white or yellow
flowers in summer,
lemon balm is very
attractive to bees.*

✼ German chamomile
*This variety of
chamomile is an
annual. The scented,
conical, yellow flowers
contain the plant's
medicinal properties.*

✼ Virginian skullcap
*Handsome and
particularly pest-
resistant, skullcap was
used by native
Americans as a
treatment for rabies.*

✼ ✼ English lavender
*There are more than 28
species of lavender to choose
from but* L. angustifolia *is
the most potent for herbal
medicinal purposes.*

INSOMNIA

To find which suits you best, try out these herbal sedatives. German chamomile calms the digestive system and combines well with hops, which contain sedative volatile oils. The poppy is a mild painkiller, while valerian promotes deep sleep without a hangover.

POT INFORMATION

Herbs

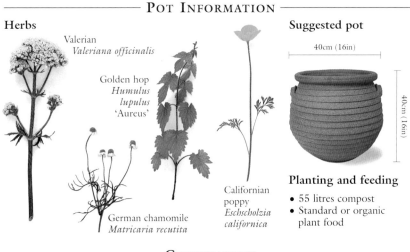

Valerian
Valeriana officinalis

Golden hop
Humulus lupulus
'Aureus'

German chamomile
Matricaria recutita

Californian poppy
Eschscholzia californica

Suggested pot

40cm (16in)

40cm (16in)

Planting and feeding

- 55 litres compost
- Standard or organic plant food

CULTIVATION

START by buying four German chamomile plants, a wild "female" hop plant, and two valerian plants from a herb specialist. Because the hop will not flower until it is at least three years old, try to buy a mature plant. Californian poppy grows readily from seed sown in spring (p.80).
POSITION in a sunny spot.
FEED every two weeks in summer.
WATER daily in hot weather.
MAINTAIN by deadheading chamomile to encourage flowering.

GATHER chamomile flowers as they open. Pick aerial parts of poppy as needed. Pick hop flowers (strobiles) when they appear, and harvest valerian root in autumn.
PROPAGATE Californian poppy and German chamomile by collecting seed in autumn and sow for plants in spring. Remove valerian and hop from the pot. Separate roots carefully. Replant hop and divide valerian (p.83). When the hop is at least three years old, propagate by pulling off a side stem with roots (p.83).

REMEDY RECIPES

Sleepy tea CAUTION (see opp.)
To treat insomnia together with headache, restlessness, and digestive upsets, make a tea with one teaspoon of dried chamomile flowers and two to three hop strobiles per cup of boiling water. Drink a cupful at bedtime.

 Deep-sleep decoction CAUTION (see opp.)
If insomnia persists, make a decoction (p.89) using a teaspoon of dried valerian root to 200ml (7fl oz) of water. Add a teaspoon of chamomile flowers. Strain. If in pain, add one teaspoon of dried poppy.

✵ Valerian
Found in damp woodland, valerian has strongly therapeutic, aromatic roots.
CAUTION
Don't use with sleep-inducing drugs.

✿ Californian poppy
Easily grown from seed, with bright orange flowers, this poppy has a very mild, and safe, narcotic effect.

✵ Golden hop
As it grows, the hop will need to be supported by twining around other plants. Papery female flowers, called strobiles, appear in late summer.
CAUTION
Don't use if depressed.

✵ German chamomile
Besides its medicinal properties, chamomile has traditionally been used as a rinse to brighten fair hair.

DEPRESSION

The dull feeling of depression can be alleviated by using these herbs. St. John's wort was a traditional remedy for melancholia, and betony restores the nervous system and relieves tension. Lemon balm and lavender have volatile oils which promote relaxation.

POT INFORMATION

Herbs

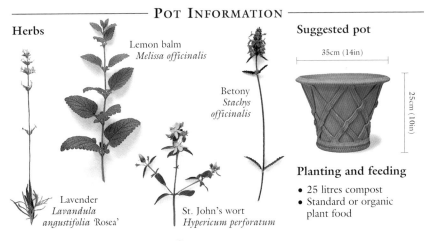

Lemon balm
Melissa officinalis

Betony
*Stachys
officinalis*

Lavender
*Lavandula
angustifolia* 'Rosea'

St. John's wort
Hypericum perforatum

Suggested pot

35cm (14in)

25cm (10in)

Planting and feeding

- 25 litres compost
- Standard or organic plant food

CULTIVATION

START by buying one lemon balm plant and three lavender plants from a garden centre. We have recommended *Lavandula angustifolia* 'Rosea' as it has attractive pink flowers. Betony and St. John's wort are only available from a herb specialist. Buy two St. John's wort and two betony plants.
POSITION in a sunny spot.
WATER daily in hot, dry weather.
FEED six weeks after planting and then regularly every two weeks until autumn.

MAINTAIN by trimming all these plants.
GATHER aerial parts of St. John's wort as the flowers appear. Gather aerial parts of lemon balm and betony as needed. Pick lavender flowers when they begin to open.
PROPAGATE lavender from cuttings (p.82). Propagate lemon balm by pulling away a few healthy, rooted pieces of stem (p.83) and replanting in the container. Detach one or two plantlets of betony and replant. Divide St. John's wort (p.83).

REMEDY RECIPES

Relaxing tea
Make a tea (p.88) with a large sprig of lemon balm to a cup of boiling water. Add one lavender flower. Drink three times a day.

Tea for a heavy head
Make a tea (p.88) with three betony leaves or three flowers to a cup

of boiling water. To shift dull headaches which can often accompany depression, take a cup in the morning, as needed.

 Cheering tincture
CAUTION (see opp.)
Make a St. John's wort tincture (p.90). Take a teaspoonful three times a day for three weeks and no more than two months.

St. John's wort
This ancient remedy for melancholia was supposed to scare away evil spirits, protecting those who planted it at their front door.
CAUTION
Prolonged use can lead to photo-sensitivity.

Lemon balm
In ancient times, lemon balm was considered the ultimate remedy for a troubled nervous system.

Betony
The Celts named this herb. "Beu", and "ton", meaning "head" and "good". It became a favourite monastery herb.

Lavender
Although herbalists prefer L. angustifolia, most species make an acceptable substitute. All are equally aromatic.

COLD SORES

Caused by viral infection and linked to stress, cold sores will respond best if treated at the first sign of irritation. Lemon balm is anti-viral, while marigold and garlic are both anti-infective. Purple coneflower has beneficial effects on the immune system.

POT INFORMATION

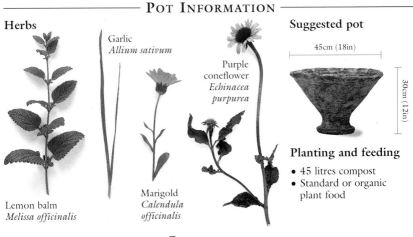

Herbs

Lemon balm
Melissa officinalis

Garlic
Allium sativum

Marigold
Calendula officinalis

Purple coneflower
Echinacea purpurea

Suggested pot

45cm (18in)

30cm (12in)

Planting and feeding

- 45 litres compost
- Standard or organic plant food

CULTIVATION

START by planting about six garlic cloves in autumn. These will produce plants the following spring. Alternatively, buy four plants in spring from a garden centre. Buy one purple coneflower and one lemon balm from a garden centre. Buy at least four marigold plants from a garden centre, or grow from seed (p.80) and aim to have at least four to plant in the container.
POSITION in a sunny spot.
WATER daily in hot, dry weather.
FEED every two weeks during the summer.

MAINTAIN by trimming lemon balm. Deadhead purple coneflower and marigold.
GATHER lemon balm leaves when needed and marigold flowers as they open. Harvest root of purple coneflower in autumn. Uproot garlic bulb in summer or autumn.
PROPAGATE lemon balm from rooted pieces of stem (p.83). Plant garlic cloves in autumn. Collect and sow marigold seed for plants the following spring (p.80). Divide coneflower when it is mature enough to provide plants for the following year (p.83).

REMEDY RECIPES

Protective decoction
Cold sores sometimes appear at times of stress. As a protective measure, make a decoction of purple coneflower root (p.89) by boiling three teaspoons of root in 500ml (17fl oz) of water. Add three marigold flowers. Cool, strain, and drink one cupful three times a day.

Lemon balm salve
Squeeze some juice from a lemon balm leaf and apply directly to the skin.

Garlic salve
Cut open a garlic clove and dab directly on to the affected area at the first sign of irritation.

✳ Purple coneflower
*The flowers of this
plant have lovely
rich-brown stamens
and purple-pink
petals. It takes
several years to grow a
fairly good-sized clump.*

✿ Marigold
*With their orange
or yellow flowers,
marigolds combine
particularly well with
purple coneflower.*

✆ Garlic
*Easily grown from a
clove, garlic has been
shown to improve
resistance to infection.*

✣ Lemon balm
*A tenacious plant with
a tendency to take over a
pot, lemon balm should be
picked liberally for use in
remedies or herbal teas to
keep it under control.*

ATHLETE'S FOOT

An irritating condition, athlete's foot is caused by a fungus that thrives in warm, damp places like those between the toes. Marigold is antifungal and antiseptic, while the three varieties of thyme have a powerful anti-microbial action.

POT INFORMATION

Herbs

Suggested pot

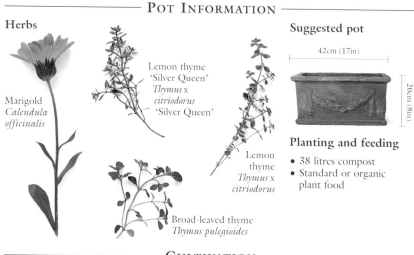

Marigold
Calendula officinalis

Lemon thyme
'Silver Queen'
Thymus x citriodorus
'Silver Queen'

Lemon thyme
Thymus x citriodorus

Broad-leaved thyme
Thymus pulegioides

42cm (17in)

20cm (8in)

Planting and feeding

- 38 litres compost
- Standard or organic plant food

CULTIVATION

START by buying the three varieties of thyme from a garden centre or specialist herb grower. Either buy six or seven marigold plants, or grow from seed in spring and plant six or seven in the pot.
POSITION in a sunny spot. All these plants can tolerate arid conditions.
WATER daily in very hot, dry weather.
FEED with a dilute solution two or three times during the summer months.

MAINTAIN by using thymes regularly; trim the plants to keep their shape. Deadhead marigold to encourage flowering.
GATHER aerial parts of thyme when needed. Pick marigold flowers as they open.
PROPAGATE all the thymes by removing from the container and dividing the rootball at the end of the season (p.83). Collect seed of marigold in autumn and sow for plants next spring (p.80).

REMEDY RECIPES

Thyme and marigold tea
To treat the condition internally, make a tea (p.88) with a sprig of one of the thymes and a marigold flower to a cup of boiling water. Drink three times a day.

Marigold cream
Gently heat three or four flowers in 30g (1oz) base cream (p.92). Stir

well until the cream turns an orange colour. Strain into a jar. Leave to cool and apply three times a day.

Marigold wash
Make a simple infusion (p.88) from the flowers, including the outer, green cup. Leave to cool and bathe the affected parts frequently with this wash.

❊ Broad-leaved thyme
This is an improved version of wild thyme. It is herbally more potent, with strongly aromatic leaves.

❊ Lemon thyme 'Silver Queen'
A relatively new variety of lemon thyme, 'Silver Queen' has random silver markings and a strong lemony scent.

❊ Marigold
Not to be confused with Tagetes *or French marigold, which is not therapeutic,* Calendula officinalis *is essential to any herb collection.*

❊ Lemon thyme
With its fine silvery leaves, lemon thyme makes an agreeable contrast with the marigold in the pot.

ECZEMA

All these plants are blood cleansers, helping to remove toxins from the body. Chickweed and fumitory are also cooling, and treat inflamed, irritated skin, while red clover helps to nourish the skin. Blue flag aids digestion and hence the elimination of toxins.

POT INFORMATION

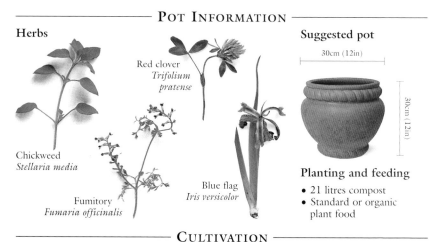

Herbs

Red clover
Trifolium pratense

Chickweed
Stellaria media

Fumitory
Fumaria officinalis

Blue flag
Iris versicolor

Suggested pot

30cm (12in)

30cm (12in)

Planting and feeding
- 21 litres compost
- Standard or organic plant food

CULTIVATION

START by buying two or three blue flag irises from a herb specialist. Also buy three plants each of fumitory and red clover, or grow them from seed and plant three of each in the pot (p.80). When these plants are in position, sow chickweed seed by sprinkling directly on to the surface of the pot, then water. These chickweed seeds should germinate in just a few days.
POSITION in a sunny spot.
WATER frequently in hot, dry weather.
FEED twice during the summer months.

MAINTAIN by deadheading irises.
GATHER red clover flowers when they bloom. Pick aerial parts of fumitory and chickweed when required, and dig up blue flag rhizome in autumn.
PROPAGATE blue flag by removing the plant from the container; cut two or three budded sections from the old rhizome and replant into the container. In spring, detach a few clover plantlets from the parent and replant (p.83). Collect and resow seed of fumitory and chickweed.

REMEDY RECIPES

Chickweed cream
Heat a large handful of aerial parts of chickweed in three tablespoons of base cream (p.92) until the cream turns green. Strain into a jar, and apply as needed. This is a good, general moisturizer. Marigold creams, washes, and oils as described on pages 34, 46, and 58 are also useful for treating skin affected by eczema.

Cleansing tea CAUTION (see opp.)
Make a tea (p.88) with two teaspoons of red clover flowers and a handful of aerial parts of fumitory. Drink three times a day for at least a month. To improve digestion and elimination, make a decoction (p.89) with ½ teaspoon of blue flag rhizome. Drink one cup daily for one month.

✹ Blue flag
This iris has delicate, lilac-blue flowers and plain, strap-like leaves. When crushed, the leaves have a sweet scent.
CAUTION
Excessive doses can cause nausea and diarrhoea.

✹ Red clover
Although often not welcome in the garden because of its invasive habit, red clover looks pretty in a pot where it can be easily restrained.

✹ Chickweed
The fresh juice of this plant can soothe itching. Simply squeeze a few leaves between finger and thumb and rub gently on the skin.

✹ Fumitory
The tiny pink flowers of fumitory are said to look like smoke, hence its Latin name, Fumaria.

ARTHRITIS OR PAINFUL JOINTS

Herbalists believe that joints become inflamed when toxins circulate
too slowly in the body. These herbs help to remedy this. Parsley and
wild carrot are blood cleansers; feverfew speeds circulation; meadow-
sweet is anti-inflammatory, and marjoram is a general stimulant.

POT INFORMATION

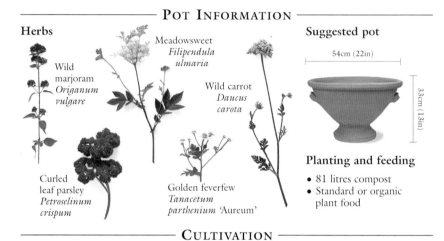

Herbs

Wild
marjoram
Origanum
vulgare

Meadowsweet
Filipendula
ulmaria

Wild carrot
Daucus
carota

Curled
leaf parsley
Petroselinum
crispum

Golden feverfew
Tanacetum
parthenium 'Aureum'

Suggested pot

54cm (22in)

33cm (13in)

Planting and feeding

- 81 litres compost
- Standard or organic
  plant food

CULTIVATION

START by buying two meadowsweet and
two wild carrot plants from a herb specialist.
Golden feverfew is widely available. One
is enough. Parsley and marjoram are also
widely available because of their culinary
popularity. Plant two each.
POSITION in partial shade.
WATER regularly and use a saucer if there
is any danger of the container drying out.
FEED monthly from mid-summer.

MAINTAIN by trimming all the plants
in the container regularly.
GATHER aerial parts of feverfew, parsley,
meadowsweet, marjoram, and wild carrot
as needed.
PROPAGATE feverfew by collecting and
sowing seed (p.80). Divide root balls of
marjoram and meadowsweet (p.83).
Collect and sow seed of biennials parsley
and wild carrot in the autumn (p.80).

REMEDY RECIPES

Feverfew for improved
circulation CAUTION (see opp.)
To mask the bitter taste of feverfew, put
a leaf between two pieces of bread and
butter. Eat daily to aid the circulation.

Diuretic tea CAUTION (see opp.)
Make a tea (p.88) with a sprig of
parsley and a sprig of wild carrot to a cup
of boiling water. Drink a cupful three
times a day to help get rid of toxins.

Anti-inflammatory tea for pain
CAUTION (see opp.)
Make a standard tea (p.88) with aerial
parts of meadowsweet. Use near boiling
water. Drink three times a day.

Cold infused oil of marjoram
Make an infused oil (p.91) using
the aerial parts of marjoram steeped in
wheatgerm oil. Rub into painful joints
to encourage blood supply to the area.

Golden feverfew
As it puts on fresh growth, the golden variety of feverfew makes a bright splash of colour early in the year.
CAUTION
• Can cause mouth ulcers.
• Avoid if taking anti-clotting drugs.

Meadowsweet
The foliage and flowers of this herb have the scent of hayfields.
CAUTION
Avoid if allergic to aspirin.

Wild marjoram
With dense, pink flowers, marjoram thrives on being cut back, producing fresh, green growth until winter.

Wild carrot
This plant has a powerful diuretic action. Although its sinewy, white aromatic roots smell like the familiar orange vegetable, they have a bitter taste.

Curled leaf parsley
There are over 30 varieties of parsley, but this parsley is considered the most useful by herbalists.
CAUTION
Avoid high doses if pregnant.

HEADACHES

Feverfew is known to have a beneficial effect on migraine, and vervain on premenstrual and nauseous headaches. Skullcap and betony are nervines, with a particular affinity for the head. Rosemary is thought to improve blood supply to the head.

POT INFORMATION

Herbs

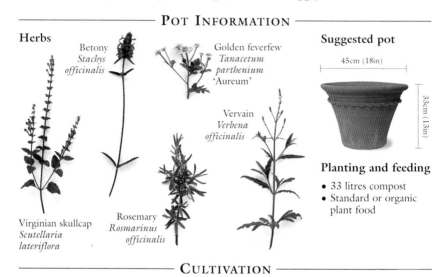

Betony
Stachys officinalis

Golden feverfew
Tanacetum parthenium 'Aureum'

Vervain
Verbena officinalis

Virginian skullcap
Scutellaria lateriflora

Rosemary
Rosmarinus officinalis

Suggested pot

45cm (18in)

33cm (13in)

Planting and feeding

- 33 litres compost
- Standard or organic plant food

CULTIVATION

START by growing feverfew from seed, or buy two plants from a garden centre. Buy one betony, one vervain, and one skullcap as plants from a herb specialist. Rosemary is widely available. Buy one large plant.
POSITION where the pot will get some shade, especially during the heat of the day.
WATER daily in hot, dry weather and particularly watch the betony and the vervain for any signs of drying out.

FEED monthly in summer.
MAINTAIN by trimming stems and dead-heading flowers. Pinch out the growing points of feverfew to encourage bushing.
GATHER aerial parts of feverfew, rosemary, skullcap, betony, and vervain as needed.
PROPAGATE betony from plantlets (p.83). Collect feverfew seed; sow for plants next spring (p.80). Take cuttings of rosemary (p.82). Divide skullcap and vervain (p.83).

REMEDY RECIPES

Tea for tension headaches
Make a tea (p.88) using leaves from one sprig of rosemary and three leaves of betony per cup of boiling water. To retain the oils, keep the pot covered. This mixture of rosemary and betony makes a relaxing tea which will clear the head. Make and drink a cupful once or twice a day to relieve tension.

Feverfew for migraine onset
CAUTION (see opp.)
At the first sign of migraine, make a tiny sandwich as described on page 38.

 Tincture for chronic headaches
Make a tincture using equal parts of vervain and skullcap (p.90). Take one teaspoonful three times a day as needed.

Betony
In the wild, betony favours damp, cool places and tends to grow against the north- or east-facing aspect of trees and shrubs.

Vervain
Dense spikes of pretty, lilac-pink flowers appear on vervain in summer. In ancient times, it was considered a holy plant by Druids and Christians alike.

Feverfew
This golden variety is delightful in a pot and is just as effective herbally as the common feverfew.
CAUTION
- *Can cause mouth ulcers.*
- *Avoid if taking anti-clotting drugs.*

Rosemary
An evergreen, aromatic shrub, rosemary has resinous, needle-like leaves. R. officinalis has mauve-blue flowers in spring.

Virginian skullcap
This herb has branching stems of oval leaves and purple-blue flowers that resemble a skullcap.

PMS AND IRREGULAR PERIODS

Both lady's mantle and white dead nettle are herbs traditionally used for women's problems. Taken over a few months, they can help regulate the menstrual cycle. Evening primrose seeds contain oils that are rich in fatty acids and reduce premenstrual syndrome.

POT INFORMATION

Herbs

White dead nettle
Lamium album

Evening primrose
Oenothera biennis

Lady's mantle
Alchemilla xanthochlora

Suggested pot

47cm (19in)

39cm (15in)

Planting and feeding

- 85 litres compost
- Standard or organic plant food

CULTIVATION

START by buying two evening primrose plants from a garden centre. Buy two lady's mantle from a herb specialist. Grow dead nettle from seed (p.80) and pot four plants.
POSITION in a sunny spot.
WATER every day in hot, dry weather.
FEED every two weeks from early summer onwards.
MAINTAIN by trimming dead nettle and lady's mantle and using in remedies. Keep evening primrose free of aphids (p.84).

GATHER aerial parts of lady's mantle and nettle as needed. Collect evening primrose seed at the end of the season (p.87).
PROPAGATE white dead nettle from a few rooted pieces of stem (p.83). Evening primrose can be propagated from seed but, because it is biennial, seed sown in autumn may not flower until the second year, so you may prefer to buy new plants. Either divide lady's mantle (p.83) or grow from seed (p.80).

REMEDY RECIPES

 Evening primrose supplement
When the evening primrose has flowered, and the seed pods formed and desiccated, cut the flower stalks and shake the seed into a paper bag (p.87). Add the seed to a pepper mill or just sprinkle directly on to food. To help combat symptoms of PMS, take ½ to one teaspoonful every day.

Tea for irregular periods
CAUTION (see opp.)
Make a tea (p.88) with one leaf of lady's mantle and a sprig of white dead nettle per cup of boiling water. Drink one cup twice a day for three months to balance the hormones. This can be made into a tincture (p.90) for winter use. Take one teaspoonful twice a day for three months.

Lady's mantle
One of a small number of plants that reproduces without fertilization, lady's mantle will seed itself quite freely.
CAUTION
Avoid if you might be pregnant.

Evening primrose
This is a beautiful plant, especially at night when its lemon-yellow, scented flowers are at their best. The seed contains a nutritional oil.

White dead nettle
Although it resembles the stinging nettle, this species does not sting, hence the common name "dead nettle".

PERIOD PAINS

As its name suggests, crampbark treats the cramp associated with menstruation. Rosemary helps by increasing the supply of blood to the uterus. Motherwort is anti-spasmodic and a good uterine tonic, while wild marjoram encourages menstrual flow.

POT INFORMATION

Herbs

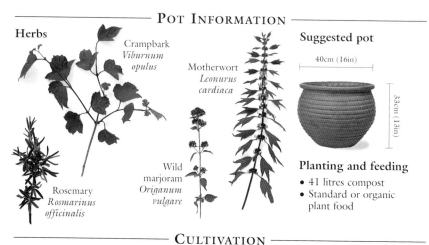

Crampbark
Viburnum opulus

Motherwort
Leonurus cardiaca

Rosemary
Rosmarinus officinalis

Wild marjoram
Origanum vulgare

Suggested pot

40cm (16in)

33cm (13in)

Planting and feeding
• 41 litres compost
• Standard or organic plant food

CULTIVATION

START by buying one crampbark plant from a garden centre or tree specialist. Buy one motherwort plant and one wild marjoram plant from a herb specialist. Buy one large rosemary from a garden centre.
POSITION where the pot will get at least half a day's sunshine every day.
WATER daily in hot, dry weather.
FEED every two weeks in summer.
MAINTAIN by pinching out the growing tips of motherwort and crampbark in spring.

GATHER aerial parts of motherwort, rosemary, and wild marjoram as required during the growing season. Use bark from twigs of crampbark after the plant has flowered in mid-summer, or later.
PROPAGATE crampbark and rosemary from cuttings (p.82). If plants are large enough, divide root balls of motherwort and marjoram in autumn and replant the healthiest pieces into the pot (p.83). This will produce plants the following year.

REMEDY RECIPES

Relaxing tea
Make a standard tea (p.88) with aerial parts of rosemary and marjoram. Drink three cups a day as needed.

Womb tonic syrup
CAUTION (see opp.)
Motherwort is more palatable taken in a syrup. Make a syrup as shown on page 89 using the leaves from two stems of

motherwort to 200ml (7fl oz) syrup. Take one teaspoonful morning and evening for three months.

Anti-cramp decoction
Make a decoction (p.89) with two teaspoons of bark of crampbark per cup of water. Bring to the boil. Simmer for 10 to 15 mins. Drink up to five cups a day before and during a period.

Motherwort
Traditionally used for treating anxiety accompanied by palpitations, this sturdy plant is a strong grower with upright stems and mildly pungent leaves.
CAUTION
Avoid in the first three months of pregnancy.

Crampbark
This common shrub is found on damp, chalky soils. The berries are toxic when raw, but in Canada, they are cooked to make a sauce.

Rosemary
All the varieties of this attractive plant grow well in containers, but it is best to use R. officinalis for medicinal purposes.

Wild marjoram
A perennial with dark-green, aromatic leaves, only the wild species of marjoram is considered potent by herbalists.

45

PREGNANCY

*These herbs ease problems in pregnancy. German chamomile helps
the digestive system cope with added demands and decreased space.
Black horehound reduces nausea. Raspberry strengthens the muscles
of the uterus, and marigold can soothe vaginal thrush.*

POT INFORMATION

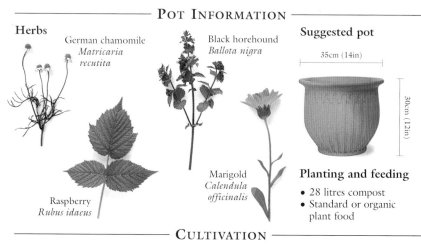

Herbs

German chamomile
*Matricaria
recutita*

Black horehound
Ballota nigra

Raspberry
Rubus idaeus

Marigold
*Calendula
officinalis*

Suggested pot

35cm (14in)

30cm (12in)

Planting and feeding

- 28 litres compost
- Standard or organic
  plant food

CULTIVATION

START by buying a wild raspberry plant
from a garden centre. (If this is not available,
buy a cultivated one.) Buy two horehound
plants from a herb specialist. Grow marigold
from seed (p.80), or buy four plants. Grow
chamomile from seed and pot four plants.
POSITION in a bright, not too sunny, spot.
WATER daily in hot, dry weather.
FEED with monthly dilute feeds.
MAINTAIN by deadheading marigold and
chamomile to encourage flowering.

GATHER marigold and chamomile flowers
as they appear. Pick raspberry leaves as
needed. Pick leaves of horehound as the
plant comes into bloom.
PROPAGATE raspberry by cutting off a few
suckers (new growth with roots attached)
and replanting in the pot at the end of the
season. Propagate black horehound by
dividing (p.83). Collect marigold and
chamomile seed in autumn and sow for
plants the following spring (p.80).

REMEDY RECIPES

Marigold wash for thrush
Make an infusion (p.88) with
two handfuls of flowers to 600ml (1 pint)
water. Steep for 15 mins. Strain and cool.
Bathe the vulva with this wash as needed.

Raspberry leaf tea
Make a tea (p.88) with three
leaves per cup of boiling water. Drink
warm three times a day for the final six

months of pregnancy to help ease
labour. Add peppermint, honey, ginger,
or lemon to vary the flavour.

Tea for morning sickness
Make a tea (p.88) with a few
chamomile flowers and two leaves of
black horehound. Stir in some honey and
leave to cool. Sip a cupful on waking and
at intervals throughout the morning.

Raspberry
Whether you buy a wild or cultivated one, this plant is unlikely to bear fruit in a pot. The leaves have been used for centuries by women preparing for childbirth.

German chamomile
Because it seems to have a beneficial effect on ailing plants, German chamomile is sometimes called the "plant's physician".

Marigold
A cold infused oil (p.91) made from this versatile plant can be rubbed into the breasts and abdomen to help prevent stretchmarks.

Black horehound
True to its Shropshire name "stinking Roger", this plant smells most unpleasant but it is, nonetheless, an effective remedy for nausea.

MENOPAUSE

These herbs are women's natural allies at this stage of their lives. Clover and sage compensate for lower oestrogen levels and lady's mantle helps rebalance the hormones. Motherwort, a uterine and blood tonic, reduces sweating, while St. John's wort treats depression.

POT INFORMATION

Herbs

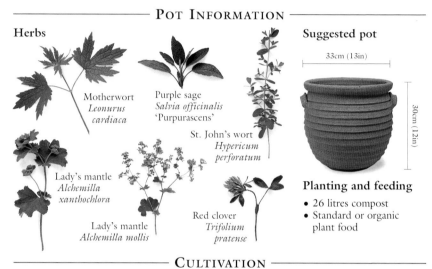

Motherwort
Leonurus cardiaca

Purple sage
Salvia officinalis 'Purpurascens'

St. John's wort
Hypericum perforatum

Lady's mantle
Alchemilla xanthochlora

Lady's mantle
Alchemilla mollis

Red clover
Trifolium pratense

Suggested pot

33cm (13in)

30cm (12in)

Planting and feeding

- 26 litres compost
- Standard or organic plant food

CULTIVATION

START by growing red clover from seed (p.80) and pot two plants. Buy one motherwort, one St. John's wort, and one *Alchemilla xanthochlora* from a herb specialist. (If you can't get *A. xanthoclora*, you can buy *A. mollis*, although it is less potent herbally.) Buy two purple sage plants from a garden centre.
POSITION in a sunny spot.
WATER frequently in hot, dry weather.
FEED monthly from mid-summer.

MAINTAIN by trimming all the plants.
GATHER red clover flowers as they appear. Pick aerial parts of St. John's wort, motherwort, and lady's mantle when in flower. Pick aerial parts of purple sage as needed.
PROPAGATE motherwort, St John's wort, and lady's mantle by dividing in autumn (p.83). Take cuttings of purple sage in summer (p.82). Detach a few plantlets of clover from the parent (p.83) and replant in the container in autumn.

REMEDY RECIPES

 Syrup for a hot flush
CAUTIONS (see opp.)
Chop up four leaves each of purple sage and motherwort. Make 100 ml (3½fl oz) of syrup with the chopped herbs (p.89). Heat for 15 mins. Leave to cool, then strain. Place in a dropper bottle and take several drops at the onset of a hot flush.

Tonic tea CAUTIONS (see opp.)
For a general tonic tea (p.88), put two teaspoons of each herb in a teapot and pour on boiling water. Allow to steep for 10 mins. Strain and drink either hot or cold. A cup of this tea can be taken up to three times a day. If symptoms persist, see your doctor.

St. John's wort
*Oil glands, which appear
as tiny perforations, can be
seen if the leaves of St. John's
wort are held up to the light.*
CAUTION
*Prolonged use can lead
to photo-sensitivity.*

Motherwort
*This plant is a strong grower.
Pinch out the topmost leaves
from each stem in late spring.*
CAUTION
Avoid high doses if pregnant.

Purple sage
*An evergreen shrub, purple
sage has reddish-purple,
textured foliage with
mauve-blue flowers which
appear in early summer.*
CAUTION
• *Avoid if epileptic.*
  • *Avoid high doses if
    pregnant.*

Lady's mantle
*Alchemilla mollis
can be used but
A. xanthochlora
is preferable.*

Red clover
*A plant that
grows best under
harsh conditions,
red clover favours
hot sunshine and
poor soil.*

Lady's mantle
*The most potent
species medicinally
is A. xanthochlora.*
CAUTION
Do not use if pregnant.

CYSTITIS

These herbs should be taken as teas to flush out the urinary system and reduce painful inflammation of the bladder. Bearberry and common juniper are antiseptics and combat infection. Heartsease and golden rod are soothing, helping to alleviate sensitivity.

POT INFORMATION

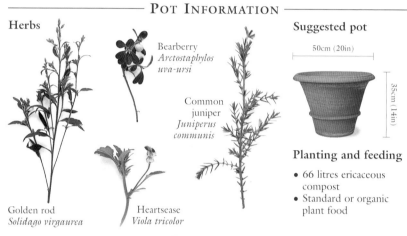

Herbs

Bearberry
Arctostaphylos uva-ursi

Common juniper
Juniperus communis

Golden rod
Solidago virgaurea

Heartsease
Viola tricolor

Suggested pot

50cm (20in)

35cm (14in)

Planting and feeding

- 66 litres ericaceous compost
- Standard or organic plant food

CULTIVATION

START by ordering one common juniper and one bearberry from a conifer or herb specialist. Buy one plant of golden rod from a herb specialist. Either buy four heartsease plants or grow from seed in spring (p.80).
POSITION where the container will get a few hours sunshine every day.
WATER only with rainwater if you live in an area with calcareous or limy soil.
FEED every two weeks from mid-summer.

MAINTAIN by trimming bearberry, golden rod, and heartsease. Leave juniper to berry.
GATHER aerial parts of golden rod and heartsease when in flower. Pick leaves of bearberry as needed. Collect juniper berries at the end of the summer.
PROPAGATE juniper by cuttings in spring (p.82). Take cuttings of bearberry (p.82) in summer. Divide golden rod in autumn (p.83). Collect seed of heartsease in autumn (p.87) and sow for plants in spring.

REMEDY RECIPES

Preventative tea
Make a standard tea (p.88) with aerial parts of golden rod and heartsease, and leaves of bearberry. Drink one or two cupfuls per day at the first signs of cystitis.

Cystitis tea CAUTION (see opp.)
Make a tea (p.88) with one teaspoon of lightly crushed juniper

berries and one handful of mixed, fresh leaves of bearberry, heartsease, and golden rod per pot of boiling water. If you are using dried material, use ½ teaspoon of crushed juniper berries and one teaspoon each of the other herbs. Drink a cupful about six times a day during an attack of cystitis. If symptoms persist, take professional advice.

❀ ✎ **Heartsease**
*In folklore, this wild pansy
was said to be a love charm,
helping lovers to win the
object of their desire.*

❀ ✎ **Golden rod**
*There are many forms of
golden rod. Make sure you get
the species* S. virgaurea *which
is the best to use medicinally,
rather than a garden variety.*

☼ **Common juniper**
*This shrub has berry-
like cones that contain
a detoxifying oil.*
CAUTION
• *Avoid if pregnant.*
• *Avoid if you have
damaged kidneys.*

✎ **Bearberry**
*The oval leaves of this
shrub are shiny. In
spring, the branches
are covered in
delicate bell-shaped
pink flowers followed
by red berries.*

BREAST-FEEDING

*Fennel seeds and aerial parts of goat's rue are both known to
aid the production of breast milk. Teas made with peppermint and
fennel pass through the mother's milk and help reduce colic in the
baby. Marigold cream eases sore nipples.*

POT INFORMATION

Herbs

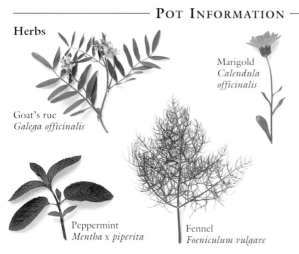

Marigold
*Calendula
officinalis*

Goat's rue
Galega officinalis

Peppermint
Mentha x piperita

Fennel
Foeniculum vulgare

Suggested pot

42cm (17in)

28cm (11in)

Planting and feeding

- 38 litres compost
- Standard or organic plant food

CULTIVATION

START by buying two peppermint, two fennel, and four marigold plants from a garden centre. Marigold can also be grown from seed (p.80). Buy one goat's rue plant from a herb specialist.

POSITION the container in a sunny spot.

WATER daily during hot, dry weather.

FEED every two weeks in summer.

MAINTAIN peppermint and goat's rue by trimming and using in remedies.

GATHER aerial parts of peppermint and goat's rue as needed. Pick marigold flowers as they open. Collect fennel seed when it forms, after the plant has flowered.

PROPAGATE goat's rue and marigold by collecting seeds in the autumn and sow for plants next spring (p.80). Also keep a few fennel seeds for sowing in spring. Propagate peppermint by detaching a few rooted pieces of stem and replanting in the pot (p.83).

REMEDY RECIPES

Tea to increase breast milk production CAUTION (see opp.)
Make a tea (p.88) using two teaspoons of lightly crushed fennel seed to one cup of boiling water. Steep for 10 mins, then strain and drink twice a day. Alternatively, use a handful of aerial parts of goat's rue. Drink one cupful twice daily while breast-feeding.

Tea to calm mother and baby
Make a tea (p.88) with a teaspoon of fennel seed and a sprig of mint to a cup of water. Drink three times a day.

Cream for sore nipples
Make a marigold cream as shown on page 92. To prevent soreness, apply to the nipples after breast-feeding.

Goat's rue
With lovely pink,
sweet-pea-like flowers
and finely cut blue-grey
foliage, goat's rue
makes a pretty
addition to a pot.
CAUTION
Diabetics should seek
professional guidance
before using.

Marigold
The traditional "pot"
marigold used by
herbalists has single or
double flowers. Double
flowers give more petals
to use in remedies.

Peppermint
Easy to grow in a
container, peppermint
has a strong taste and
an invigorating,
revitalizing effect,
making it an ideal tea
for nursing mothers.

Fennel
This familiar culinary
herb has a tall habit
and should be grown
in a large container.
The foliage, flowers,
and seed all smell
strongly of aniseed.

SLEEPING PROBLEMS

All gentle relaxants, the herbs in this pot are particularly suitable for babies. The remedies can be given in a bottle either alone, or diluted with fruit juice. Catmint and German chamomile also help reduce fever and colic.

POT INFORMATION

Herbs

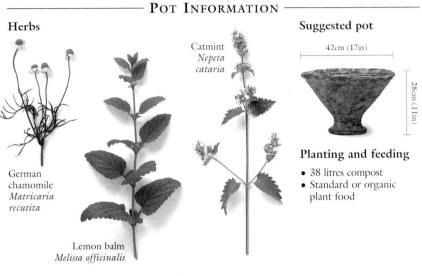

German chamomile
Matricaria recutita

Lemon balm
Melissa officinalis

Catmint
Nepeta cataria

Suggested pot

42cm (17in)

28cm (11in)

Planting and feeding

- 38 litres compost
- Standard or organic plant food

CULTIVATION

START by growing German chamomile from seed (p.80). Plant as many as five into this container. Buy one catmint from a herb specialist. Lemon balm is widely available from garden centres; you will only need one plant.
POSITION in a sunny spot.
WATER daily during hot, dry weather.
FEED in early summer and then every three weeks throughout the growing season.
MAINTAIN by trimming all these plants. Deadhead chamomile to encourage

flowering. In early summer, pinch out the topmost growing points of each stem of catmint and lemon balm to encourage these plants to bush out.
GATHER aerial parts of lemon balm and aerial parts of catmint as needed. Pick German chamomile flowers as they appear.
PROPAGATE lemon balm and catmint from a few rooted pieces of stem (p.83). German chamomile seed can be collected (p.87) in autumn and sown for plants the following spring (p.80).

REMEDY RECIPES

Tea to help baby sleep
Experiment with the herbs in this pot to see which one suits your baby best. Make a tea (p.88) with a small sprig of lemon balm or catmint or a teaspoon of

chamomile flowers. Strain and leave to cool. Dilute with 50 per cent water or fruit juice and give in a bottle. Breast-feeding mothers can drink the tea to relax themselves and the baby.

❀ **Lemon balm**
A strong grower, with lemon-scented leaves, this herb's Latin name, "melissa", comes from the Greek for "honey bee", indicating its attractiveness to bees.

❀ **Catmint**
This herb is known to attract cats and repel rats. Its spikes of aromatic pinky-white flowers are also rather popular with bees.

❀ **German chamomile**
The delicate foliage of the chamomile makes a pleasing contrast to the coarse leaves of catmint and lemon balm in this container.

TUMMY PROBLEMS

*Many babies have colic, which is spasm in the stomach or intestines.
German chamomile has a gentle, anti-spasmodic effect on the
digestive system. Fennel is carminative and was used as an
ingredient in gripe water. Agrimony is a mildly astringent tonic.*

POT INFORMATION

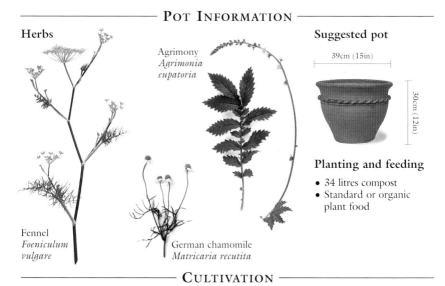

Herbs

Agrimony
*Agrimonia
eupatoria*

Fennel
*Foeniculum
vulgare*

German chamomile
Matricaria recutita

Suggested pot

39cm (15in)

30cm (12in)

Planting and feeding

- 34 litres compost
- Standard or organic
  plant food

CULTIVATION

START by buying one fennel plant from
a garden centre. Grow German chamomile
from seed (p.80). Plant four in the pot.
Agrimony is available from herb specialists.
Buy two plants.
POSITION this container where it will
receive quite a lot of sunshine.
WATER daily in hot, dry weather.
FEED every two weeks from early summer
onwards, throughout the growing season.

MAINTAIN by deadheading chamomile.
GATHER aerial parts of agrimony as
needed, and German chamomile flowers
as they appear. Collect fennel seeds as they
form, after the plant has flowered.
PROPAGATE German chamomile by
collecting and sowing seed (p.80). Keep
some fennel seed and sow for plants next
spring. Divide root ball of agrimony at
the end of the season (p.83).

REMEDY RECIPES

Anti-gripe tea
This tea is quite safe for colicky
babies and can be diluted with 50 per
cent water and given in a bottle. Make
a tea (p.88) with a teaspoon of crushed
fennel seed plus three or four chamomile
flowers to a pint of water. Let it stand for
ten minutes. Strain and give when cool.

Tea for a tummy upset
Make a tea (p.88) with one small
fresh agrimony leaf to a cup of boiling
water. Leave to steep for 15 mins. Strain
and then leave to cool. Give to the baby
twice a day in a bottle. If the baby's
symptoms persist, seek professional
advice as soon as possible.

Fennel
Fennel has deep roots and this makes it prone to drying out in a pot, so make sure it has sufficient water.

Agrimony
This herb contains a yellow dye which was traditionally used in the process of tanning leather.

German chamomile
As well as aiding digestion, chamomile tea helps a baby to sleep.

NAPPY RASH

Comfrey and marigold are renowned healers of skin conditions and are suitable for a baby. Comfrey heals skin so fast that it should not be used on infected skin, since it might seal in the infection. Heartsease is soothing, and useful for treating inflamed skin.

POT INFORMATION

Herbs

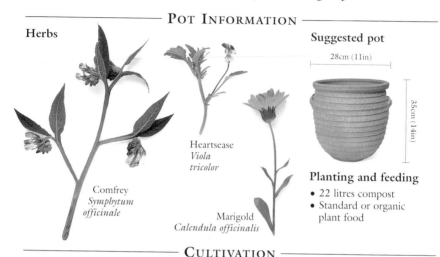

Heartsease
*Viola
tricolor*

Comfrey
*Symphytum
officinale*

Marigold
Calendula officinalis

Suggested pot

28cm (11in)

35cm (14in)

Planting and feeding
- 22 litres compost
- Standard or organic plant food

CULTIVATION

START by buying two comfrey plants from a herb specialist. Grow marigolds and heartsease from seed (p.80) or buy them as plants from a garden centre. Aim to have at least four of each for planting.
POSITION the pot where the plants will receive half a day's sun.
WATER frequently in hot, dry weather. Do not allow the comfrey to dry out.
FEED monthly throughout the summer.

MAINTAIN by deadheading marigold to encourage flowers. Remove large or ragged comfrey leaves and compost them.
GATHER aerial parts of comfrey as needed and aerial parts of heartsease as the flowers appear. Pick marigold flowers as they open.
PROPAGATE comfrey by trimming the root ball to a few young roots. These will produce new plants. Collect marigold and heartsease seed (p.87) and sow for plants next spring.

REMEDY RECIPES

 Comfrey ointment
CAUTION (see opp.)
Make a hot infused oil as shown on page 91. Make an ointment by melting 15g (½oz) of beeswax into 200ml (7fl oz) of comfrey oil (p.92). Stir well. When the wax has melted, pour into jars and allow to cool. This ointment will protect the baby's skin. Apply on clean skin each time the nappy is changed.

Soothing marigold oil
Fill a jar with marigold flowers. Pour over wheatgerm oil to cover. Seal and leave on a sunny windowsill for a month. Strain. Apply to skin as needed.

Heartsease wash
Make an infusion (p.88) with a handful of aerial parts to a cup of boiling water. Cool to rinse the baby's bottom.

Comfrey
This is an eye-catching plant, with large, hairy leaves and delicate flowers that range in colour from white to pink to blue.
CAUTION
Do not apply to infected wounds.
See also page 7.

Marigold
The Latin name for marigold, Calendula, *comes from* calends, *or* months, indicating the plant's ability to flower nearly all year.

Heartsease
A delightful and delicate violet, heartsease always sports three colours, purple, yellow, and white, hence its Latin name tricolor.

TEETHING AND EARACHE

Marsh mallow root contains a soft mucilage which soothes the irritated, inflamed gums of teething babies. German chamomile is relaxing and carminative, and a traditional remedy for restlessness in infants. Black mullein has a beneficial effect on earache.

POT INFORMATION

Herbs

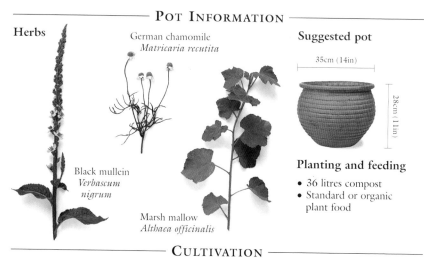

German chamomile
Matricaria recutita

Black mullein
Verbascum nigrum

Marsh mallow
Althaea officinalis

Suggested pot

35cm (14in)

28cm (11in)

Planting and feeding

- 36 litres compost
- Standard or organic plant food

CULTIVATION

START by growing chamomile from seed (p.80). You will need three plants. Buy marsh mallow and black mullein plants from a herb specialist. One plant of each is enough but several look more attractive.
POSITION in light shade with some sun.
WATER frequently in hot, dry weather.
FEED monthly from early summer.
MAINTAIN by deadheading chamomile and trimming marsh mallow after flowering.

GATHER mullein flowers as they open. Pick German chamomile flowers as they appear. Harvest marsh mallow root in autumn.
PROPAGATE marsh mallow by dividing in autumn (p.83). Black mullein can be grown from seed (p.80) but, because it is biennial, seed sown in autumn may not flower until the second year, so it may be better to buy new plants. Collect and sow chamomile seed in autumn for plants next spring.

REMEDY RECIPES

 Teething sticks
Cut and wash a 5–7cm (2–3in) piece of marsh mallow root and dry. Trim off side shoots and peel away the bark. Give to the baby to chew.

Teething ointment
Fill a small jar with chamomile flowers; pour on a small amount of syrup (p.89). When a tooth is coming through, strain, and rub very sparingly on the gum.

 Calming tea
Make a standard tea (p.88) with chamomile flowers. Leave to cool. Dilute with equal parts of water. Give in a bottle.

Cold infused oil for earache
Make an cold oil with mullein flowers (p.91). Strain and bottle. Put two drops in the ear three times a day.

✳ **Marsh mallow**
This pretty plant has tall flowering stems, velvety leaves, and white or pink flowers with purple stamens. It does not flower until late summer.

✳ **Black mullein**
Mullein has long spikes of bright yellow flowers which open randomly along the stems.

✳ **German chamomile**
Similar in effect and appearance to Roman chamomile, the flowers contain vital minerals and vitamin A.

CUTS AND BRUISES

These herbs treat minor skin injuries. Yarrow staunches bleeding, comfrey draws tissue together and promotes growth. Marigold is an all-purpose antiseptic, while arnica disperses internal bleeding and is ideal for treating bruises.

POT INFORMATION

Herbs

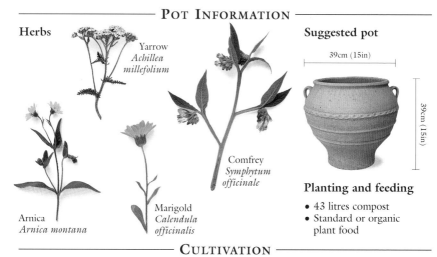

Yarrow
Achillea millefolium

Comfrey
Symphytum officinale

Arnica
Arnica montana

Marigold
Calendula officinalis

Suggested pot

39cm (15in)

39cm (15in)

Planting and feeding

- 43 litres compost
- Standard or organic plant food

CULTIVATION

START by growing all these herbs from seed (p.80). Alternatively, buy three or four marigold plants from a garden centre and two arnica plants, one yarrow, and one comfrey plant from a herb specialist.
POSITION in partial shade.
WATER often during hot, dry weather. If the yarrow is flagging, put a saucer beneath the pot, so no water is wasted.
FEED six weeks after planting and then monthly throughout the summer.

MAINTAIN by removing large or ragged comfrey leaves and composting them.
GATHER comfrey and yarrow leaves as needed. Pick marigold and arnica flowers as they appear.
PROPAGATE comfrey by removing all but a few roots from the pot. These will produce new plants. Propagate arnica by dividing (p.83). Replant rooted stems of yarrow (p.83). Collect and sow marigold seed for plants the following spring (p.80).

REMEDY RECIPES

 Ointment for clean cuts and bruises CAUTION (see p.7)
Dry six or seven comfrey leaves in a very slow oven. Make a hot infused oil (p.91); use it to prepare an ointment (p.92).

Marigold cream
To make a marigold cream, follow the instructions given on page 92.

Oil for bruises and sprains
CAUTION (see opp. and p.7)
Make two infused oils (p.91): one of arnica flowers and one of comfrey leaves. Combine in equal parts and apply.

Yarrow juice to stop bleeding
Rub a few soft leaves together and apply the juice to the skin.

Comfrey
Sometimes referred to as "knitbone", comfrey is a large, handsome plant with blue, white, or pink flowers.
CAUTION
See page 7.

Marigold
Unequalled as a skin healer, this herb has yellow to orangey-red flowers that bloom almost all year round.

Arnica
Found naturally in subalpine areas, arnica is a pretty plant with yellow, daisy-like flowers which appear in summer. It thrives in cool conditions.
CAUTION
Do not apply to broken skin or take internally.

Yarrow
Also known as staunchweed, yarrow is prized by herbalists. Other plants seem to benefit from growing near this herb.

STINGS AND BURNS

Houseleek contains a jelly-like fluid which soothes minor stings and burns, while St. John's wort heals burns. Lemon balm contains anti-oxidant oils to reduce inflammation. Ribwort and selfheal are antidotes for insect stings and bites.

POT INFORMATION

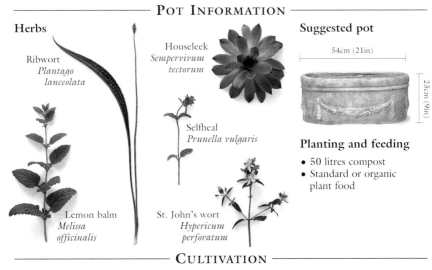

Herbs

Ribwort
*Plantago
lanceolata*

Houseleek
*Sempervivum
tectorum*

Selfheal
Prunella vulgaris

Lemon balm
*Melissa
officinalis*

St. John's wort
*Hypericum
perforatum*

Suggested pot

54cm (21in)

23cm (9in)

Planting and feeding

- 50 litres compost
- Standard or organic
  plant food

CULTIVATION

START by growing ribwort from seed. Plant two in the container. Buy one self-heal plant and one St. John's wort plant from a herb specialist. Buy two houseleek plants and one lemon balm plant from a garden centre.

POSITION the container where it will receive some sun and some shade.

WATER every two days in hot, dry weather.

FEED monthly during the summer.

MAINTAIN by trimming lemon balm during the growing season.

GATHER aerial parts of houseleek, ribwort, and lemon balm when needed, and flowering tops of St. John's wort when they form. Pick aerial parts of selfheal as the plant flowers.

PROPAGATE St. John's wort by dividing (p.83). Replant rooted stems of selfheal and lemon balm, and detach plantlets of ribwort and houseleek and replant (p.83).

REMEDY RECIPES

Fresh juice for stings or burns
Pick a houseleek, lemon balm, or ribwort leaf, crush and rub the juice directly on to the wound.

Dressing for burns
Mix juice from a houseleek leaf with a teaspoon of honey. Spread on a clean piece of lint and tape in place.

St. John's wort oil for burns
CAUTION (see opp.)
Make a cold infused oil (p.91). Apply to area of burned skin, as needed.

Sting and burn cream
Make a cream (p.92) with equal quantities of fresh or dried aerial parts of ribwort, lemon balm, and selfheal.

Lemon balm
A generous herb, lemon balm provides leaves all through the summer. If kept in a temperature above 8°C (43°F), it will produce leaves in the winter too.

St. John's wort
Several species of St. John's wort exist, but only H. perforatum is used by herbalists.
CAUTION
Do not go out in the sun with this oil on your skin.

Ribwort
This species of plantain has thin, ribbon-like leaves and erect flower stems which can grow very tall.

Houseleek
Although resembling a cactus, this herb is totally hardy. Its leaves contain a mucilage which can be rubbed straight on to the skin.

Selfheal
The name of this pretty plant indicates its long history of first-aid use.

Hangover

Prevention is better than cure. Milk thistle tea taken before drinking alcohol in excess helps protect the liver from toxic stress. Lavender helps to settle the stomach and dispel the depression that often follows over-indulgence. Mugwort is a general tonic.

Pot Information

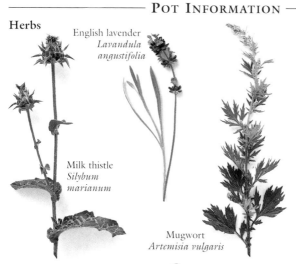

Herbs

English lavender
*Lavandula
angustifolia*

Milk thistle
*Silybum
marianum*

Mugwort
Artemisia vulgaris

Suggested pot

30cm (12in)

28cm (11in)

Planting and feeding
- 20 litres compost
- Standard or organic plant food

Cultivation

START by growing milk thistle from seed or buy two plants from a herb specialist. Buy two mugwort plants from a herb specialist. Buy at least two lavender plants from a garden centre.
POSITION in a sunny spot.
WATER daily during hot, dry weather.
FEED this pot weekly from early summer onwards with a half-strength fertilizer.
MAINTAIN by trimming mugwort and lavender regularly. If the milk thistle leaves

start to turn yellow, give the plants more water, and spray with a dilute feed.
GATHER aerial parts of mugwort as needed. Collect milk thistle seed as it forms. Pick aerial parts of lavender just before the flowers open.
PROPAGATE milk thistle by keeping a few seeds and planting in the pot in spring (p.80). Take cuttings of lavender during the growing season (p.82) and divide mugwort in autumn (p.83).

Remedy Recipes

Preventive milk thistle tea
Make a tea (p.88) by putting one teaspoon of milk thistle seed per cup of water in a saucepan and boiling for 10 mins. Strain and drink hot. Take a cup of this tea three times during the day before going to a party.

Liver tea CAUTION (see opp.)
Make a pot of tea (p.88) with a handful of mugwort leaves. Strain.

Tea for the morning after
Make a pot of tea (p.88) with three lavender sprigs. Strain. Drink a cup.

❀❦ Wormwood
A beautiful plant with finely cut leaves and lime-green bauble flowers, wormwood was once used to make the apéritif absinthe.
CAUTION
Do not use if pregnant.

❧ Peppermint
In common with all mints, peppermint is invasive, so it is best grown in a pot and the leaves used frequently in herbal teas.

❀❦ Black horehound
A plant with a rampant habit, black horehound has hairy stems, heart-shaped leaves, and small purple flowers in summer.

❀ German chamomile
This variety of chamomile grows very easily from seed. The seed looks like fine dust and germinates very quickly (p.80).

NERVOUS TONIC

Borage is a tonic for the glands which produce adrenalin, and thus helps us to deal with stress. Rosemary and lavender are known for promoting relaxation and counteracting depression. Rose hips are rich in vitamin C which keeps the body healthy.

POT INFORMATION

Herbs

Borage
Borago officinalis

Dog rose
Rosa canina

Rosemary
Rosmarinus officinalis

English lavender
Lavandula angustifolia

Suggested pot

42cm (17in)

40cm (16in)

Planting and feeding

- 55 litres compost
- Standard or organic plant food

CULTIVATION

START by buying two rosemary plants, two lavender plants, and one borage plant from a garden centre. The dog (or wild) rose can be bought from a herb specialist.
POSITION in a sunny spot.
WATER frequently in hot, dry weather.
FEED weekly with a dilute solution, six weeks after planting.
MAINTAIN by trimming the lavender and rosemary. Treat any aphid infestation on the rose with soft soap.

GATHER aerial parts of borage and rosemary as needed. Pick aerial parts of lavender just before the flowers open. Harvest rosehips when they form from late summer onwards.
PROPAGATE rosemary and lavender by taking cuttings (p.82). Propagate the rose by removing seed from desiccated hips and sowing (p.80). (Plants take up to three years to grow.) Collect and sow seed of borage for plants next spring.

REMEDY RECIPES

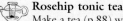 **Rosehip tonic tea**
Make a tea (p.88) with about three or four rosehips to one cup of boiling water, then strain well. Drink daily.

 Borage tincture
CAUTION (see p.7)
Pick enough aerial parts to fill a small jar. Make a tincture by covering with

a mixture of alcohol and water (p.90). This makes a gentle tonic which can be diluted in a little warm water and taken three times a day when stressed.

Lavender and rosemary tea
Make a tea (p.88) with a sprig of each herb to a cup of boiling water. Take a cupful every day as needed.

☾ **Dog rose**
This species of wild rose is a familar sight growing through hedgerows in northern temperate zones.

❀ **Borage**
Also known by the name "star flower", borage will grow very tall, and flower happily in a pot.
CAUTION
See page 7.

❀ **English lavender**
If the pungent flowering tips are not available, the evergreen leaves can be used very effectively in remedies.

❀ **Rosemary**
A sprig of rosemary placed under a child's pillow is said to prevent nightmares.

CHOLESTEROL CONTROL

Garlic, wild garlic, and chives all belong to the allium, or onion, family. Known for their anti-infective properties, they also enhance the body's ability to digest fats. Southernwood, a hardy perennial, improves the liver's ability to break down fats.

POT INFORMATION

Herbs

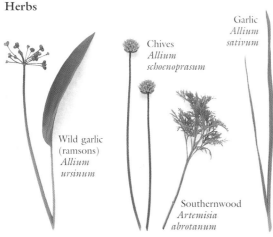

Garlic
*Allium
sativum*

Chives
*Allium
schoenoprasum*

Wild garlic
(ramsons)
*Allium
ursinum*

Southernwood
*Artemisia
abrotanum*

Suggested pot

28cm (11in)

28cm (11in)

Planting and feeding

• 17 litres compost
• Standard or organic plant food

CULTIVATION

START by planting six garlic cloves in autumn, or buy four plants from a garden centre in spring. Buy one wild garlic from a herb specialist. Buy two chive and two Southernwood plants from a garden centre.
POSITION in a shady spot.
WATER frequently in early spring, when the wild garlic is in flower.
FEED monthly throughout the summer.
MAINTAIN by trimming leaves of chives, wild and cultivated garlic. Pinch out topmost growth of southernwood to help maintain its shape.
GATHER aerial parts of southernwood as needed. Pick chives and wild garlic leaves when they appear. Unearth garlic bulbs for use in late summer.
PROPAGATE southernwood by cuttings in spring or early summer (p.82). The chives and wild garlic will quickly multiply in the pot. Replant new garlic cloves in autumn for plants the following summer.

REMEDY RECIPES

 Southernwood tea
CAUTION (see opp.)
Southernwood has a strong, exotic flavour. To stimulate the liver and improve digestion, make a tea (p.88) using one sprig to one cup of boiling water. Drink a cup of hot tea before each main meal.

Garlic and chive syrup
Chop up two wild garlic plants, or three cloves of cultivated garlic, and two or three chives. Make 250ml (8fl oz) of syrup (p.89) and add the chopped herbs. Cool, strain, and bottle. Take one teaspoonful three times a day before meals.

🌿 Chives
Chives have pretty lilac flowers on long, green stems. The hollow, onion-flavoured leaves aid digestion and can be used liberally in salads and as a garnish for other cold dishes.

🌿 Garlic
Familiar as a popular culinary herb, garlic can be easily grown from one clove.

🌿 Southernwood
Traditionally combined with lavender and box to edge the borders of herb gardens, this aromatic herb has finely cut silvery leaves. Small, yellow, rather unexceptional flowers appear in summer.
CAUTION
Do not use if pregnant.

🌿 Wild garlic
The wild species grows naturally in damp woodland. It bears star-shaped white flowers which form attractive green seedheads.

VITAMINS AND MINERALS

*Parsley is a blood cleanser and source of vitamin C and iron.
Alfalfa contains many vitamins and minerals including zinc, an
anti-inflammatory, which is also present in coltsfoot. Nettle and
dock are both traditional tonics because they are rich in iron.*

POT INFORMATION

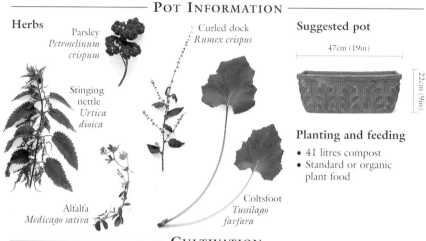

Herbs

Parsley
Petroselinum crispum

Stinging nettle
Urtica dioica

Alfalfa
Medicago sativa

Curled dock
Rumex crispus

Coltsfoot
Tussilago farfara

Suggested pot

47cm (19in)

22cm (9in)

Planting and feeding

- 41 litres compost
- Standard or organic plant food

CULTIVATION

START by buying alfalfa, dock, nettle, and coltsfoot seed from a herb specialist. Sow alfalfa and coltsfoot into seed trays in spring. Transfer to the pot when 10cm (4in) tall. Sow nettle and dock seed directly into the pot. Buy four parsley plants from a garden centre in spring and plant in the pot.
POSITION in a shady spot.
WATER daily in summer.
FEED every two weeks in summer.

MAINTAIN by trimming nettle. Pinch out topmost points of alfalfa for bushy growth.
GATHER aerial parts of coltsfoot, nettle, and parsley as needed. Collect alfalfa seeds as they form. In autumn, harvest dock roots.
PROPAGATE coltsfoot, dock, and nettle by root cuttings (p.83). Propagate alfalfa by keeping a few seeds and sowing for plants next year (p.80). Collect and sow seed of parsley, a biennial, in its second year.

REMEDY RECIPES

Nutritious alfalfa sprouts
Soak a tablespoon of seed in four tablespoons of water overnight in a jar. Pour off water. Leave in the dark to sprout for three days, rinsing twice a day. Sprouts can be eaten in salads and sandwiches.

Cleansing tea CAUTION (see opp.)
Make a pot of tea (p.88) with nettle leaves. Drink three times a day.

Tonic tea CAUTION (see opp.)
Make a tea (p.88) with a coltsfoot leaf and a large sprig of parsley per cup of water. Take a cupful three times a day.

Dock tonic syrup
Chop 30cm (12in) of root. Boil in 500ml (17fl oz) of water for 15 mins. Add 300g (10oz) of sugar. Stir to dissolve. Strain. Take a teaspoonful daily.

Alfalfa

Although capable of sending roots deep down into the soil, from where it extracts nutrients, alfalfa will grow happily within the restrictions of a pot. It has pretty, pink, clover-like flowers.

Coltsfoot

Because of its unusual habit of producing the rather dull, yellow flowers before the rosette-shaped leaves, coltsfoot is sometimes called "son before father".
CAUTION
See page 7.

Stinging nettle

Young nettle tops can be used to make nutritious soups. Fortunately, they lose their sting when boiled.
CAUTION
Wear gloves and use extreme caution around this plant.

Curled dock

This much-disliked weed with its tiny, unspectacular flowers is rich in nutrients. Just eating a leaf will give you a large amount of iron.

Parsley

This popular culinary species has densely curled leaves.
CAUTION
Avoid high doses if pregnant.

IMMUNE SYSTEM STIMULANT

These herbs stimulate the body's own defences. Coneflower increases the activity of scavenging white blood cells and false indigo increases the body's ability to resist infection. Marigold helps support the lymphatic system, while hemp agrimony is a general tonic.

POT INFORMATION

Herbs

Coneflower
*Echinacea
angustifolia*

Marigold
*Calendula
officinalis*

False indigo
*Baptisia
australis*

Hemp agrimony
*Eupatorium
cannabinum*

Suggested pot

39cm (15in)

28cm (11in)

Planting and feeding

- 35 litres compost
- Standard or organic plant food

CULTIVATION

START by buying two coneflower plants and two hemp agrimony plants from a herb specialist. Buy one false indigo plant from a hardy plant or herb specialist. Buy marigold as plants, or grow from seed (p.80). You will need three plants.
POSITION in a sunny spot.
WATER daily in hot, dry weather. Don't allow the coneflower to droop.
FEED with half-strength solution every two weeks during the summer.

MAINTAIN by deadheading marigold and coneflower to encourage flowering.
GATHER marigold flowers as they open. Pick aerial parts of hemp agrimony before the flowers open. Harvest roots of false indigo and coneflower in autumn.
PROPAGATE agrimony from rooted pieces of stem (p.83). Collect marigold seed and sow for plants next spring (p.80). When coneflower and indigo are mature enough, propagate by division (p.83).

REMEDY RECIPES

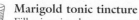 **Decoction for infections**
Make a decoction (p.89) with two teaspoons of coneflower root and one of false indigo root. Simmer for ten mins. Strain. Drink a cupful three times a day.

Marigold tonic tincture
Fill a jam jar three-quarters full with marigold flowerheads and pour over enough vodka to cover. Allow to stand for one month. Strain and bottle. Take one teaspoonful three times a day.

Tonic tea
Make a tea (p.88) with aerial parts of hemp agrimony. Drink a cupful three times a day, whenever you feel that you might be vulnerable to infection.

✵ Coneflower
*Similar in appearance and
effect to purple coneflower
(p.12), this species is
probably more potent.*

✿ Hemp agrimony
*A common roadside plant
in temperate zones, hemp
agrimony has tall stems which
bear pink flower clusters.*

✵ False indigo
*When grown from seed,
this herb takes several years
to flower. Make sure you
buy one that has been
propagated by division. It
should flower in its second
year, with blue flowers that
develop into huge seed pods.*

✳ Marigold
*The flowerheads of
this herb contain the
highest concentration
of the plant's medicinal
properties. They can be
dried easily (p.86).*

GROWING HERBS AND MAKING REMEDIES

The main methods of growing and propagating herbs – by seed, cuttings, and dividing – are shown in step-by-step illustrations on pages 80–83. Guidelines on how to plant up a pot are given on pages 84–85. Pages 88–92 show how simple herbal remedies can be made with standard kitchen equipment.

PROPAGATION

*Propagating is a most satisfying part of tending plants. Before the
end of the growing season, collect seedheads and take cuttings.
At the end of the autumn, empty the pot: take root cuttings,
divide root balls, and replant perennials and shrubs.*

SOWING SEED

This method is used for annuals, such
as German chamomile (shown here).
Whether you buy seed or collect it
from your own plants, the method is
the same. If seed trays can be protected
from frost, sow seed in autumn for
planting out in spring, otherwise sow
as early as possible in spring.

1 Fill a seed tray with a seed-sowing
medium or vermiculite. Firm lightly
and evenly and water thoroughly.

2 Sow seed on the surface. If the seed is
very fine, use a folded piece of card
and tap gently to scatter the seed evenly.

*Remember to label the
seed tray once sown.*

3 Cover the surface with a fine layer of
seed-sowing medium or vermiculite.
Position in a light, draught-free spot out
of direct sun. Check daily and keep the
medium moist by watering with tepid
water from a fine-rosed watering can.

4 After three to four weeks, when the
seedlings are just big enough to handle,
fill as many small pots as you need plants
with potting compost. Firm the surface
about 3cm (½in) below the rim of each pot.
Make a hole in the compost with a dibber.

5 Gently tease out the strongest of the seedlings from the tray, using a widger or teaspoon. Always handle the seedlings by their two open leaves.

6 Carefully insert a seedling in each of the prepared pots. Ease in the roots with the dibber, then gently firm the compost around the seedling. Label.

Strong top-growth indicates chamomile is ready for planting in the container.

7 Place the potted seedlings on a drip tray and water with a fine-rosed watering can. Place in a light spot, away from draughts. Check seedlings daily and keep the growing medium moist.

8 When the seedlings have developed more leaves, and the roots begin to fill the pot, they should be planted out into bigger pots. If they have been in a warm place indoors, expose them gradually to outdoor temperatures, once the danger of frost has passed.

TAKING CUTTINGS

Propagation by cuttings is the best method for shrubby plants such as lavender, rosemary, thyme, and southernwood. Cuttings should be taken from non-flowering shoots during the growing season. Leave to root and grow on, and plant out in a container the following spring.

1 Select four or five healthy stems. Cut off pieces of stem about the length of a finger with scissors or small secateurs.

2 Pull off all but the topmost foliage to leave a bare stem. Make a clean cut across the stem just below a leaf joint.

3 Dibble the cuttings around the edge of a 14cm (5½in) pot of a half and half grit-and-vermiculite mixture. Water. Leave in a light, draught-free place. After 2–4 weeks, gently pull at a cutting. If you feel resistance, roots have formed; if not, leave for a week.

4 Pot on each rooted cutting into a 9cm (3½in) pot of growing medium; label. Overwinter in a sheltered position. In spring, the cuttings should be ready for planting in the container. If the plants were in a warm place, harden off before planting out.

ROOT CUTTINGS

The stock of some hardy perennials such as horseradish, comfrey, and elecampane can be increased by taking root cuttings. Do this in the autumn to obtain plants for the following spring. Remove the parent plant from the container and trim off some healthy roots with scissors.

1 Cut four or five finger-length sections of root with a sharp knife, making an angled cut at the end farthest from the plant.

Place cuttings in potting medium or vermiculite.

2 Dibble the cuttings, angled end first, into holes around the edge of the pot. Water, label, and put out of direct sun and draughts. Keep moist.

PLANTLETS

Betony, plantain, Roman chamomile, and lady's mantle all form young plants around the base of the parent plant. When you empty the pot at the end of the growing season, gently detach these plantlets from the parent rootball. Pot up, water, and keep in a sheltered position until next spring.

Gently tease out the roots of each plantlet as you detach it.

ROOTED STEMS

Some plants like mint and ground ivy produce new roots and shoots from stems during the growing season. Cut these root-bearing stems from the parent. Pot up rooted stems of pot-bound plants like the one below, and compost the parent plant.

Choose a healthy stem with strong roots.

DIVIDING A ROOT BALL

Hardy perennials like coneflowers take several seasons to mature. When they do become too large, lift and divide them. Shake the soil from the roots and cut through them to obtain two or more sections. Replant to grow into good-sized plants for next year.

Use a large, sharp knife to cut through the root ball.

MAKING UP A POT

Besides looking attractive, containers are a convenient way of growing some invasive plants such as peppermint, coltsfoot, and nettles, which would otherwise spread quickly through open soil and soon become a nuisance in the garden.

Growing medium

Container plants need a well-balanced growing medium (compost), based on soil or a peat substitute, with lots of organic matter. You can buy ready-made compost or make your own. A dark, crumbly soil, not sticky clay, is best. The quantities below will fill a 40cm (16in) by 30cm (12in) deep pot.

- 1 bucket (18 litres) sieved garden soil
- ¼ bucket horticultural grit or sharp sand
- ¾ bucket leaf mould or garden compost
- 1 tablespoon bonemeal
- 1 dessertspoon seaweed meal
- 1 dessertspoon calcified seaweed

Sieve the soil and spread in a circle, 80cm (32in) in diameter, near the pot. Spread the other ingredients evenly over the soil. Draw into a heap. Fill the pot with the compost.

Watering

Regularly soak the soil with a watering can or hose during the growing season.

Feeding

The nutrients in any compost will need replenishing six weeks after planting, and regularly in the growing season. Any standard plant food can be used, but organic feeds such as seaweed extract or liquid residue from a worm composter are preferable for herbs.

Maintaining

Trim off excessive growth during the growing season. Flowers that have not been picked for use in remedies or for drying should be deadheaded so more flowers will form. Watch out for aphids; spray them with a solution of soft soap, available from garden centres.

DESIGNING A POT

Remember to decide where you want to position your container, whether in full or partial sun or shade, before filling it with compost and plants. It will be quite heavy to move afterwards.

1 Assemble the plants. Put a few small stones over the drainage hole in the pot and half-fill with compost.

2 Choose a large perennial plant for the centre of the planting so it can have as much root space as possible. Tap it out of its pot, tease out the roots a little, and place it on the compost surface.

3 Add enough compost to fill three-quarters of the pot. Use a trowel to make hollows in the compost around the central plant and insert the other plants, with the larger-growing plants at the back.

Lemon balm

Betony

St. John's wort

Lavender

4 Insert the smaller plants at the front of the container. Finish off by filling with more compost around the plants, leaving 2.5cm (1in) below the rim for watering. Gently firm in the plants by pressing the compost with your fingers.

5 Label the plants in the finished container and water the container well with a fine-rosed watering can. Make sure that the water reaches the compost and does not just stream off the leaves. Water twice a day for the first week after planting.

MAKING REMEDIES

Herbal remedies are easy to make using standard kitchen equipment. As well as taking advantage of the growing season's abundance to make fresh remedies, lay in a store of remedies for the winter months when many plants will be dormant.

GATHERING AND STORING

Gather herbs on a sunny day and when completely dry. Pick flowers when fully open and aerial parts when flowers begin to show. Harvest roots and bulbs in autumn when the pot is emptied. Dry as much as you can. Fresh herbs can also be kept in plastic bags for a short time in the freezer.

DRYING

Like vegetables, herbs are best used fresh, but they can be dried and then stored in airtight containers away from direct sunlight for later use. Most herbs will keep in this way for up to six months. When using dried herbs, remember to use half the quantity recommended for fresh herbs.

Flowers

1 Pinch off, or use scissors to cut off dry, unblemished flowerheads at noon when the flowers are fully open. If picking marigold flowers, make sure that the green cup around each flower is retained.

Suspend drying herbs with string from a bamboo cane or stick.

2 Place the flowers in a clean paper bag. Close the top loosely to protect the flowers from dust, and tie with the end of a length of string or twine.

3 Hang up the bag in a warm, airy place such as an airing cupboard until the flowers are crisp.

Leaves and aerial parts

1 Pick several stalks with fresh leaves. Tie the stalks together. Hang the bunch upside-down in a dry, airy place, out of direct sunlight.

2 When the leaves have dried out and are crisp, strip them off the stalks on to a flat piece of card. Crumble up the leaves.

3 Place in a dark, airtight jar and store. Very moist leaves such as those of comfrey, borage, and plantain are best dried slowly in a warm oven for about two hours, then crumbled and stored.

Seed

In autumn, seed can be collected for use in herbal remedies and to propagate annuals such as chamomile and marigold. Cut off the flower stalk when the seed has formed and is desiccated. To collect the seed, hang the stalks upside-down over a tray. Alternatively, a paper bag could be tied around the bunch of stalks to catch the seed.

Put a tray underneath to collect the falling seed.

Roots

1 After removing the root from the plant, soak in cold water for about one hour to remove soil and dirt. Scrub clean. Cut through large roots and trim of any excess.

2 Cut into small pieces on a chopping board. Place in a paper bag. Keep in a warm, airy place until thoroughly dried. Store in an airtight container.

TEA

Also called an infusion or tisane, a tea is a simple way of using fresh or dried herbs in remedies or tonics. Herbal teas can be drunk hot or cold and can be kept for 24 hours. For a standard tea, use two teaspoons of fresh leaves or flowers or one teaspoon of dried herbs to each cup of boiling water.

1 Put fresh sprigs or leaves or some dried plant material (see above) into a teapot and pour over boiling water. Leave to steep for at least 10 mins.

An average teapot holds about 600ml (1 pint).

2 Place a tea strainer over a cup to catch the steeped herbs and pour. Strain the rest of the tea; store in a cool place.

To avoid contamination from tannin, use different teapots for herbal and Indian tea.

One cup infusion

A single cup of tea can be made either in a special tisane cup (below) or by using a tea strainer over a cup.

1 Place the strainer over the cup. Put a teaspoon of dried herbs in the strainer and pour on freshly boiled water to fill the cup. Place a lid over the cup and strainer.

2 Leave the fresh or dried herbs to steep in the cup for about 10 mins, then carefully remove the lid and the strainer. The tea is now ready to drink.

SYRUP

Syrup is very comforting to take and therefore a good medium for soothing remedies. If making syrup for a baby under one year, do not use honey.

1 Make a tea (p.88) with 150g (5oz) herbs and 600ml (1 pint) water. Steep for 20 mins. Strain into a pan, add 375g (¾lb) sugar or honey, and stir slowly over heat until syrupy. Cool.

Use the herb chopped or whole.

2 Pour into glass bottles. Use cork stoppers to seal as screw-top bottles can explode if syrup ferments.

DECOCTION

Extracting the active constituents of tough plant material, such as roots and bark, requires a more vigorous action than the gentle infusion method that is used for teas and tisanes (p.88). Decoctions should be made fresh on the day of use but they can be kept for up to 24 hours.

The residue can be composted after use.

1 Place chopped roots or bark in a saucepan and add cold water. Use two teaspoons of fresh, or one teaspoon of dried, herbs per cup of water. Bring to the boil; simmer for 15–20 mins. The liquid should reduce by one-third (see inset).

2 Strain the decoction through a sieve into a jug. Cover and allow the liquid to cool before drinking. Store any surplus in a cool place for use later in the day.

TINCTURE

Sometimes it is quicker and more convenient to take a spoonful of medicine than to make a tea or decoction. Tinctures are made by steeping herbs in alcohol. The alcohol extracts the active constituents of the herbs and preserves them for up to two years. Vodka is probably the best kind of alcohol to use for making tinctures because it is tasteless.

Pour the alcohol over the fresh herb.

1 Put 125g (4oz) dry or 300g (10oz) fresh herbs into a large screw-top jar. Pour over 600ml (1 pint) 30 per cent proof (60^0) vodka. Seal the jar.

2 Leave to steep in a warm place for one month. Shake the jar well every day.

3 After a month, strain the mixture through a jelly bag into a jug. Discard or compost the remains of the herbs.

4 Pour the tincture through a funnel into a clean, dark bottle and store until the remedy is required.

COLD INFUSED OIL

Flowers and soft parts of herbs can be made into cold infused oils. These may be used as bases for ointments (p.92) or in massage and bath oils.

Secure the jelly bag to the jar with string or an elastic band.

1 Fill a large screw-top jar with tightly packed flowers or leaves. Pour over enough vegetable or olive oil to cover. Screw on the lid and stand on a sunny window-sill for one month. Shake the jar daily.

2 Strain the mixture through a jelly bag into a jug. Gather up the residue in the jelly bag and squeeze out remaining oil. Pour the liquid through a funnel into a dark bottle. Store in a cool, dark place.

HOT INFUSED OIL

This method of infusing oils is quicker than cold infused oils (see above) and more suitable for moist, juicy herbs such as borage. When making hot infused oil, use 600ml (1 pint) vegetable oil for 250g (8oz) of dried herbs. Infused oils can be stored in a cool, dark place for up to a year.

1 Place the herbs and oil in glass bowl over a simmering water.

2 Heat very gently for three hours. Strain through a muslin bag.

3 Collect the liquid in a jug and pour into a dark, sterile bottle.

OINTMENT

Ointments are made with hot or cold infused oil and beeswax, and they are good for nourishing the skin, as in nappy rash, or for strains and sprains.

1 Pour 105ml (3½fl oz) infused oil (p.91) into a glass bowl. Place over a saucepan of boiling water.

2 Add a 1cm (½in) square of beeswax and stir the liquid until the wax has completely melted.

3 While still warm, pour into dark ointment jars. Leave to set in a cool, dark place. Keep for up to a year.

CREAM

Creams are an emulsion of oil and water, easily absorbed by the skin. A convenient way of making it is to buy an emulsifying cream from a chemist and heat the plant material in it.

2 Remove from the heat. Strain through muslin or a jelly bag. Squeeze to extract all the liquid before the cream sets.

3 Leave to cool, then use a small palette knife to fill small, dark storage jars with cream. Keep for up to a year.

1 Melt two tablespoons of emulsifying cream over a low heat. Add two teaspoons dried or fresh herbs. Stir until cream takes on the colour of the herb.

PROPAGATION CHECKLIST

The plants on pages 10–77 are listed by Latin name below. All are hardy and most of the shrubs, sub-shrubs, and perennials can be left in the pot for more than one season. The easiest propagation method for each plant has been given.

Latin name	Plant type	Propagate by/from	Latin name	Plant type	Propagate by/from
Achillea millefolium	Perennial	Rooted stems	*Linum perenne*	Perennial	Seed
Agrimonia eupatoria	Perennial	Dividing	*Matricaria recutita*	Annual	Seed
Alchemilla (spp.)	Perennial	Dividing	*Medicago sativa*	Perennial	Seed
Allium sativum	Perennial	Cloves	*Melissa officinalis*	Perennial	Rooted stems
Allium schoenoprasum	Perennial	Dividing	*Mentha* x *piperita*	Perennial	Rooted stems
Allium ursinum	Perennial	Dividing	*Nepeta cataria*	Perennial	Rooted stems
Althaea officinalis	Perennial	Dividing	*Oenothera biennis*	Biennial	Seed
Arctostaphylos uva-ursi	Shrub	Cuttings	*Origanum vulgare*	Perennial	Dividing
Arnica montana	Perennial	Root cuttings	*Petroselinum crispum*	Biennial	Seed
Artemisia abrotanum	Sub-shrub	Cuttings	*Plantago* (spp.)	Perennial	Plantlets
Artemisia absinthium	Perennial	Dividing	*Polygonatum multiflorum*	Perennial	Root cuttings
Artemisia vulgaris	Perennial	Dividing	*Potentilla anserina*	Perennial	Plantlets
Ballota nigra	Perennial	Dividing	*Prunella vulgaris*	Perennial	Rooted stems
Baptisia australis	Perennial	Dividing	*Ranunculus ficaria*	Perennial	Dividing
Borago officinalis	Annual	Seed	*Rosa canina*	Shrub	Seed
Calendula officinalis	Annual	Seed	*Rosmarinus officinalis*	Sub-shrub	Cuttings
Chamaemelum nobile	Perennial	Plantlets	*Rubus idaeus*	Shrub	Suckers
Cochlearia armoracia	Perennial	Root cuttings	*Rumex crispus*	Perennial	Root cuttings
Daucus carota	Biennial	Seed	*Salvia* (spp.)	Perennial	Cuttings
Echinacea (spp.)	Perennial	Dividing	*Sanguisorba officinalis*	Perennial	Dividing
Eschscholzia californica	Annual	Seed	*Scutellaria lateriflora*	Perennial	Dividing
Eupatorium cannabinum	Perennial	Dividing	*Sempervivum tectorum*	Perennial	Plantlets
Filipendula ulmaria	Perennial	Dividing	*Silybum marianum*	Annual	Seed
Foeniculum vulgare	Perennial	Seed	*Solidago virgaurea*	Perennial	Dividing
Fumaria officinalis	Annual	Seed	*Stachys officinalis*	Perennial	Plantlets
Galega officinalis	Perennial	Seed	*Stellaria media*	Annual	Seed
Geranium robertianum	Annual	Seed	*Symphytum officinale*	Perennial	Root cuttings
Glechoma hederacea	Perennial	Rooted stems	*Tanacetum parthenium* 'Aur.'	Annual	Seed
Hamamelis virginiana	Shrub	Cuttings	*Thymus* (spp.)	Perennial	Dividing
Humulus lupulus 'Aureus'	Climber	Dividing	*Trifolium pratense*	Perennial	Plantlets
Hypericum perforatum	Perennial	Dividing	*Tropaeolum majus*	Annual	Seed
Hyssopus officinalis	Perennial	Cuttings	*Tussilago farfara*	Perennial	Root cuttings
Inula helenium	Perennial	Root cuttings	*Urtica dioica*	Perennial	Root cuttings
Iris versicolor	Perennial	Root cuttings	*Valeriana officinalis*	Perennial	Dividing
Juniperus communis	Evergreen	Cuttings	*Verbascum nigrum*	Biennial	Seed
Lamium album	Perennial	Rooted stems	*Verbena officinalis*	Perennial	Dividing
Lavandula (spp.)	Sub-shrub	Cuttings	*Viburnum opulus*	Shrub	Cuttings
Leonurus cardiaca	Perennial	Dividing	*Viola tricolor*	Annual	Seed

(spp.), meaning species, indicates that more than one species of a plant has been recommended.

INDEX

94

Glossary

Aerial parts The parts of the plant above ground.
Anti-inflammatory Reduces inflammation.
Annual Plant that lives and dies in one year.
Anti-fungal Reduces growth of fungal infections.
Anti-infective Reduces growth of bacteria.
Anti-spasmodic Reduces spasm or cramp.
Antiseptic Inhibits growth of bacteria.
Aromatic Contains volatile oils.
Astringent Contracts organic tissue.
Biennial Takes two years to set seed, then dies.
Carminative Reduces flatulence.
Colic Spasm in the stomach or intestines.
Detoxification Process of getting rid of poisons.

Ericaceous Plant that needs acid soil.
Gelatinous Soothing, jelly-like fluid.
Immune system Body's own defence system.
Inflammation Redness or swelling.
Laxative Stimulates and eases bowel action.
Mucilaginous Contains sticky, viscous sap.
Mucous membrane Tissue that secretes mucus.
Nervine Soothing nervous excitement.
Perennial Plant that produces new growth yearly.
Sedative Calms and reduces nervous tension.
Shrub Perennial plant with woody stem.
Tannin Substance that dries excess mucus.
Volatile oil Active aromatic oils in plants.

Authors' acknowledgments

The authors would like to thank Arne Herbs, Limeburn Nurseries, Limeburn Hill, Chew Magna, Avon BS18 8QW, and Poyntzfield Herb Nursery, Black Isle, Dingwall, Ross-shire, Scotland IV7 8LX.

Effie Romain would like to thank Ann Baker, Diana Baker, Daisy Benn, Maire Cussen, Jane Dunning, Lesley Freed, Heather Jones, Judy Kemp, Clare Monro, Jesse Romain, and Janet Skinner.

Sue Hawkey would like to thank Christine Hawkey, Tom Kendall, and Simeon Smith.

Publisher's acknowledgments

Dorling Kindersley would like to thank the following for lending pots for photography: Amphora, Shepherd's Bush, pp.13, 33, 43 and 55; Chelsea Gardener, Chelsea, pp.25, 41 and 53; Clifton Nurseries, Little Venice, pp.17 and 63; Hode Pottery, Canterbury, pp.11, 29, 39, 49, 59 and 71; Jon Fisher, p.15; Patio Pots, Dulwich, pp.19, 21, 31, 47 and 77. Thanks also to Frances Richardson for hand modelling; Karen Ward, Annette O'Sullivan, and Robert Ford for design assistance; Sarah Ashun for photographic assistance; Annelise Evans and Sarah Prest for editorial assistance; Sarah Ponder for the artworks; and Hilary Bird for the index.